FOLK TALES FROM CALDERDALE

PLACE LEGENDS AND LORE FROM THE CALDER VALLEY

VOLUME ONE

John Billingsley

⊙ northern earth ⊙

Folk Tales From Calderdale:
Place Legends and Lore from the Calder Valley
Vol. 1

Published by
Northern Earth
10 Jubilee Street, Mytholmroyd, Hebden Bridge
West Yorkshire HX7 5NP

ISBN 987 0 948635 02 9

First published 2007
2nd edition 2008

© John Billingsley 2007

*John Billingsley asserts the moral right
to be identified as the author of this work.*

Cover illustration:
Stoodley Pike overlooking the upper Calder valley

Printed in England by Booksprint

All rights reserved. No part of this publication may be reproduced, stored in a retrieval system, or transmitted, in any form or by any means, electronic, mechanical, photocopying, storage or otherwise, without the prior permission of the author/publisher.

Contents

Acknowledgements

Introduction…...5

Map…..9

1. The Witches of Eagle Crag…..10

2. The Cliviger Boggart…..19

3. The Bride Stones…..23

4. The Eve Stone…..30

5. Stoodley Pike…..33

6. Great Rock…..39

7. Tom Bell's Cave…..44

8. The Miller's Grave…..50

9. Churn Milk Joan…..55

10. Places and Traces….64

   Here Be Dragons - The Devil and some spurious saints - Boggarts and their like - Threats and curses - Making fun - Stones and stories

11. Endwords...87

Acknowledgments

It is easy to forget, in a world of books and TV, that we still tell each other stories, and these stories can take us in directions we may not expect. When I moved to the Calder Valley, I did not anticipate one day to be writing a book like this. Thus, when I heard stories and legends I rarely noted down who told each version to me, when and where, like a good folklorist should.

So I cannot thank every one of my informants individually - I never even knew the names of some of them, having met them while out walking or sharing a drink in a pub. Some names I do recall are Mike Haigh, Kim Parkinson, Steve Marsden, David Greenwood, Dave Hamer, Steven Beasley, Mike Haslam, Max Sunderland, and Alf and other regulars from the late-lamented Mount Skip Inn. Members of the Mytholmroyd and other local historical societies have also given me precious information. To all of those people who have passed on their tales and fragments of local lore over the last twenty-five years, my thanks are due; and not just *my* thanks, but *our* thanks, for keeping the tradition alive.

Without doubt, had I spent more time in pubs, I am sure I would have gathered more stories, so I can only urge readers to remember those local stories they hear and jot them down as they heard them when they get home, with the date, place and source, and we can work together towards building up a fine collection of local stories. I already have in progress a second volume of traditional local legends, but I would be delighted to hear any more tales that anyone would like to share with me - perhaps ghosts, or fairies, or significant events? Equally, I am ready to hear of any errors or omissions, so feel free to have your say - see p.88!

Acknowledgement is also due to Calderdale Libraries, themselves guardians of much of our traditional local lore, and the British Library, whose services are invaluable to delvers in dusty books; and to Bob Trubshaw, for general publishing advice; and to Hebden Bridge Local History Society for providing two old photographs. I am also fortunate in having the friendship of Mike Haigh, who has generously and regularly made his extensive antiquarian library and research notes available to me when I have been grappling with hard-to-find information.

Thanks also go to everybody at 'Tales at the Wharf', Hebden Bridge's excellent storytelling venue, who have been occasional guinea pigs of my attempts to keep these stories in the oral tradition. And especial appreciation to those with whom I could have spent more time, were it not for the writing....

JB

INTRODUCTION

"The legend takes shape and substance as you pass,
a strong happening, not to be denied, that still lives on"[1]

Every district has its memorable places, and every district has its stories. Invariably, they coincide, and the upper Calder valley is no exception to this pattern. This book is a collection of place legends from upper Calderdale; it is not, however, a book of local folklore, as place legends like these are just a small part of the wealth of customs, stories, beliefs, festivals, rituals, sayings, language and other handed-down knowledge circulating in communities past and present. The book consists of a retelling of local legends, put into an appropriate context of folkloristics and local history, with a concluding chapter rounding up some stray fragments of place lore that augment the folkloric record of the Calder valley. Volume 2 will follow a similar pattern of retelling and investigation.

Conditions in the upper Calder valley are amenable to the development of folklore. Its communities are long-established and, though distinct, are in easy contact with each other. The extensive web of packhorse trails and footpaths between centres and peripheries of settlement, in turn linking the local residents with the outside world, are evidence that this *de facto* communications network has been extant for centuries - conditions that are just right for the fluid circulation of stories, customs and local lore.

An extra bonus, for our purposes, is a landscape which lends itself to distinctive places, like the Bridestones and Great Rock, around which the collective imagination of succeeding generations tends to crystallise into legends. These are not just stories of something which happened, or is said to have happened, at such-and-such a place - the place itself is in some way characterised by the tale, its nature recognised and identified so that sometimes it feels as if we do not know whether the story was first told by the people or by the place. These are, in the words of the artist Paul Nash, 'authentic places' with a power to stir the imagination, and their interplay with their human neighbours makes another 'Place' - P̲eople, L̲andscape A̲nd C̲ultural E̲nvironment.

The stories which grow up around such spots are the means by which a community literally 'knows its place'; and they become the landmarks of children's formative maps, that in time become adult knowledge passed on to the next generation. By this means, place legends combine with folklore and history to construct a 'cognitive map' in the local mind, a map whose landmarks are not just significant places, but events, real and embroidered. Until the land is storied, it remains imperfectly inhabited.

However, this pattern of transmission inevitably means that place legends, like all folklore, are vulnerable, especially to patterns of population movement. Migration away from a place frequently means that that place loses a degree of relevance to one's life, however strong the emotional ties may be; migration may thus become a metaphor for the loss of place memory and identification. Rural communities all over Yorkshire and elsewhere have suffered loss of folklore (and thus the loss of an important part of their 'cultural environment') when people move away, perhaps in search of employment, or when the local community is 'displaced' by second-home ownership or those with a commuter lifestyle. Urban neighbourhoods face the same prospect when an industry, perhaps clothing or coal-mining, goes to the wall, though usually the significant places of an urban community are less natural than architectural and are understandably more transient than features of the landscape. In any such situations, however, the social power of place becomes less potent. The continuity of local transmission through generations is breached, as there are naturally fewer people to tell the tales to, since so many of the newer community will lack the overall local context in which the tales are framed.

Calderdale has fared better than many rural areas in this respect, perhaps, as the major demographic change occurring in the 1970s (the so-called 'hippie influx', itself destined for a place in the folklore archive as well as social history) was the arrival of people intending in general to make their homes and livelihoods in the area. Nevertheless, lore is not transmitted across generations as much as between successive generations, and however settled the upper valley population may now be, inevitably its inheritance of the area's old lore can only have been a fraction of that of preceding generations.

Local historians can tell us much about the documented lives of our predecessors, the built environment and more besides, but it is to folklore that we must look to acquire an idea of their everyday beliefs and lifestyles, the popular culture that underlies historical processes. Recently I read a local guidebook which referred to one of the legends we have here, and concluded that it was "probably no more than local folklore". This is a common phrase, but I find the trivialising implication of 'no more than' rather sad! Folklore is not a trivial matter, but an essential part of everyday living, permeating every aspect of our lives. It puts the flesh on the bones of history and infuses it with humanity - and place legends take it a step further. Frequently the places they memorialise are the sites of local historical memory, but just as frequently they are the haunts of extraordinary beings. Just as the places themselves are out of the ordinary, so are those that we may meet there. Place legends tell us where we'll meet fairies and boggarts, where to see a ghost, where the Devil walked, what Robin Hood got up to and the exploits of other local characters whose obituaries will never appear in local newspapers. These are not fantastic stories - a legend is defined as a story told *as if* true, and our latter-day rationalism is surely too young yet for us to dismiss accounts of beings that have been believed in for far longer than they have been scoffed at.

I have only included legends and other pieces of folklore where the story is connected with or identifies a place. Stoodley Pike, for example, is not named after any legend, but features as a key element in the tale of Great Rock and as a recognised locale for spooky goings-on, and its legends reflect this curious atmosphere; by contrast, the Miller's Grave is specifically identified by its legend.

The tales here are collected from a variety of sources, written and oral. I was surprised to find just how much of the material I first heard from an oral source, i.e. from someone's mouth rather than a printed page, and it is an indication that oral transmission, even in this age of print and Internet, is still a viable dynamic.

Any story comes with a 'voice' - either the narrator, or a persona adopted by the narrator for the sake of the story, or a mixture of both. In this collection, I have opted to vary the 'voices' of the tales, rather than adopt a single narrative approach, partly because this option seems to me to express the variety of backgrounds and perspectives from which the legends emerge - chronological, cultural, topographical, etc. Partly, also, it reflects a personal taste, in that I sometimes find my interest flagging in collections where a reteller of legends has adopted a uniform voice.

Sources, oral and textual, have been cited fully where available, saving much time for the reader who would like to pursue them further! However, in my early days in the Calder valley I neglected to note down the names of my informants, never expecting at the time that I would come to write a book like this; while I regret being unable to credit their contributions, it is true that folk tradition is invariably an anonymous stream. There are often variations of a tale, and where I have come across such variants I have noted them in the text.

So, given that legends like these often have variants, which is the correct one? This is unanswerable. Every narrator will tell a story in their own way, building upon the version that they themselves have heard. Variants are inevitable. However, every story has key motifs - episodes or images within it that contain the essential meaning - and in traditional cultures it is held to be incumbent upon narrators to maintain those key motifs, whatever embroidery they might make in the linking passages. These motifs form the essential kernel of a narrative, and without them the import of the whole is depleted. I have here tried to keep to this traditional pattern. There is no 'correct' version, and the original version may be irretrievable, but there is an incorrect version, and that is a story where the teller has deliberately altered the key motifs, whether to make it a 'better' story for their audience or to make it fit in with their personal beliefs or aims. I hope I have maintained my own principles here by neither adding nor changing any part of the key motifs of the stories, although I have padded out the bits between the key motifs, as will be obvious.

I have also tried to keep these stories in a style that can be told and retold, with individual adaptations of course, rather than put them in a 'readerly' form. I hope readers will think I have been successful in this attempt; most of these tales have been told to an audience in roughly the form presented here. Another hope of mine is that this publication will encourage people to return these legends to swim in the common pool of local stories, to be told and retold whenever an appropriate context occurs, and to be recalled whenever the place is seen, passed or talked about.

These stories, it must also be said, are not purely for entertainment - each one of them has a meaning to be drawn. Stories have morals, just like people - but, just like people's morals, sometimes you have to search them out a bit.

As an 'offcumd'n', not one who has grown up in the valley but only moved here in 1975, I am obviously not privy to the full wealth of the valley's folklore; yet as an outsider, as it were, I have the advantage of novelty, of finding an interest in local cultural history and tradition that those who grew up with it as an everyday humdrum companion may never have thought worthy of recording. Believe me, it *is* worthy. Perhaps we all need a second, objective, opinion to know what makes us special.

In the end, then, I make no apology for being an 'offcumd'n' writing about local history and tradition, and hope that readers will contact me with more stories, traditions and other lore from the Calder valley, for future generations to savour; or tell me of sources I may have missed. Nowadays I keep better source references and correspondents will be assured of a credit in forthcoming publications!

John Billingsley, February 2007

1. Halliwell Sutcliffe, The Striding Dales, Fredk. Warne, n.d., p.131

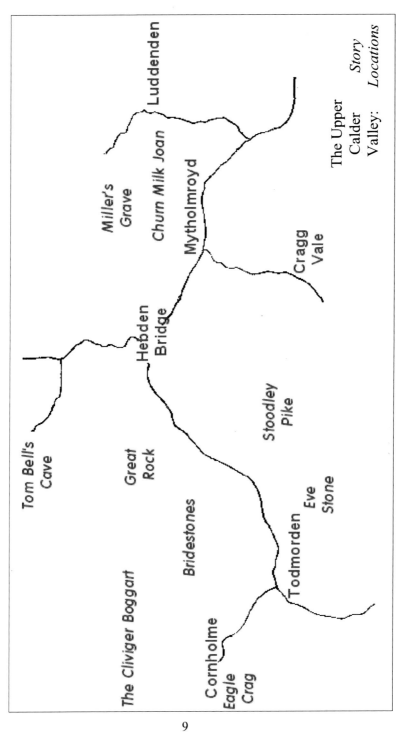

1.

THE WITCHES OF EAGLE CRAG

As you enter Cornholme on the A646 Todmorden-Burnley road, a series of bends takes you through a narrow choke of the valley. On the left, at the top of the steep bank overlooking the Staff of Life Inn, a rock outcrop juts into the dizzy heights. From most angles, you don't need a leap of the imagination to see a giant eagle soaring into the air from its rocky eyrie, and hence its name - Eagle Crag. If you're there at midnight on Hallowe'en, there's a chance you'll see a vision of the spirit world - a white doe standing on the tip of the crag, facing a hunter and his dogs.

This crag and this vision are the focal points of the area's strongest witch tale, a story which resounds through other local magical sites.

> *In Portsmouth, which today is the last village before the valley becomes Lancashire, a narrow road twists and turns up from the valley into the lonely moors. Along this road, which was old even at the time this story happened, stands a solitary farm known as Bearnshaw Tower. Rumour had it that there was a treasure buried under the tower. Over the years so many people went looking for it that they dug the foundations far enough away that one day the whole thing collapsed, and that's why there's no Bearnshaw Tower there now, just an ordinary house.*
>
> *But one sort of treasure there certainly was, in the person of its heiress, Lady Sybil. She had inherited the house and lived there alone, save for the housemaid and the farmworkers. She was unmarried and, apart from the rumours of buried treasure, was thought to be well enough off to continue in that state for some time at least. That suited her just fine, as living in such a lonely place you get to acquiring certain individual habits, and Sibyl was not at all sure that she could*

share some of her lifestyle. And she also wasn't quite ready to give up her inheritance to some husband's family, as the law required in those days. So, whenever single men came treasure-hunting her way, she sent them away again.

The most persistent of her suitors was surely William Towneley, of Hapton Tower. He was one of the rich family that had a fancy house and scores of acres on the edge of Burnley, and were never averse to acquiring more. It is certainly true that the family did have its eye on the Bearnshaw land, as it did the whole of the Cliviger valley, particularly since there appeared little chance of a male heir appearing there; and it is true too that William was young enough in the family not to have a right to any substantial claim on the family lands. Still, Sybil was easily comely enough for the young man to fall in love without any such base incentive, and he did.

Successive appeals to love, neighbourliness, reason, logic and economics all failed, however, as Sybil continued to rebuff him. And as he idly mentioned her name in passing conversations, as lovers do, he began to hear more and more rumours of her very singular personality. She was too fond of her own company, all agreed; and she was also too fond of long walks on the moors on her own; sometimes she wouldn't be seen at the house for a day and a night at a time, but everyone was sure she had no lover, though many a suitor had come and gone. There were darker stories of her being mixed up with a group of women that people were pretty sure were witches, and sometimes she had 'funny turns'. Not that anyone would come out and call her a witch, but William could easily tell what they were thinking. But it didn't put him off. Instead it gave him an idea.

You know the saying 'set a thief to catch a thief'? Well, it doesn't just have to be about thieves, and William took himself off to old Mother Helston, an old lady in the neighbourhood who made a living of sorts making up remedies for the sick of body or heart, and telling fortunes. It was said she knew how to see things hidden to most people, and people of all classes came visiting, usually after dark. They called her a cunning woman rather than a witch, but they all knew there wasn't much difference if she got angry. William wasn't the first Towneley to call on the old lady, but he was the first one to ask her advice on how to procure the hand of Lady Sybil and he offered the poor woman good reward.

So in her parlour William listened as Mother Helston confirmed that Lady Sybil really was one familiar with the magical arts, but he wasn't convinced by her recommendation to leave well alone. Perhaps, as a man of his time, his resolve was even strengthened, and he saw a chance to make a good woman of her with a Towneley marriage and Christian salvation. There was no holding his determination, and finally the old lady gave him this advice:

"You go out hunting on All Hallows Eve" she said, "just you and your dogs. Take a rope made of white silk and make sure your way takes you across Thieveley Moor at twilight. Be ready for whatever befalls and do not shirk the hunt. I shall help you if I can. And we shall see what comes to pass."

So a few weeks later William gathered his hounds, mounted his horse and rode out in the afternoon towards Thieveley Pike. The dogs picked up the odd rabbit, chased a couple of squirrels, but raised no other prey until the sun had set and they were ambling back across the moor. Suddenly a strange dog, white with chestnut-brown ears, joined the pack, and the other dogs seemed to accept the new arrival immediately. And very soon the new dog picked up a scent, sounded, and off the pack ran - and from a thicket and away across the moor sprang a milk-white doe. "Be ready for whatever befalls" recalled William...

Well, William had a good horse and his hounds were fit, but they could not catch up with the doe. All round the moor as twilight turned to a bright moonlit night she led them, but however tired they all were William remembered what he had been told - "do not shirk the hunt" - and kept his horse and hounds at it.

It must have been midnight when the panting doe suddenly stopped and faced them. She was standing on a slab of rock, and as William came closer he saw that beyond the rock there was no land - just a sheer drop into the dark valley below. The doe was hesitant and shaking on the edge of the crag - should she jump off and trust to providence? Should she run through the pack and trust her speed could evade the hounds' jaws? But the strange dog moved forward and stared into the doe's eyes, and she seemed to calm down; William urged his horse forward and took out the silken noose... and when he was close enough he tossed it lightly over the doe's head.

The doe followed William meekly as he led her away from the crag and along the top of the valleyside, and down to Bearnshaw Tower, for he was by now pretty sure of his quarry. The strange dog slipped away into the night, and soon after Mother Helston unlatched unlatched her front door and revived her fire.

At Lady Sybil's home, William took his horse and the doe into the stable, and waited. And sure enough it was not long before the white doe seemed to grow hazy, and then suddenly he was looking at Sybil, staring straight into his eyes with resentful defiance.

"Well, lady, I am sorry to discover you in this state, and I feel bound to remind you of the poor view the law takes of witches and those who change their form by night. Yet the love I feel for you will not permit me to tell of this night to anybody - should you agree to marriage with me and to put aside these dangerous ways. And surely you could do far worse than this".

So it was that Lady Sybil of Bearnshaw Tower, the area's most sought-after but elusive prize, finally accepted a suitor and was married in Holme Chapel not so long after. William, now enjoying her land as his *own, allowed her a good measure of independence and for a year or so the marriage went well and even a child was born. Sibyl was careful to avoid suspicion, but still occasionally walked abroad at night, often in the form of a cat, slipping in and out of people's houses and barns and enjoying the company of the night until light began to grow, when she slipped back to her bed.*

Now, the people at nearby Cliviger Mill were not hostile to cats, as they were always useful to keep the rats and mice down, but there was one cat they didn't much care for. It was milk white, and only came at night and seemed to spend more time nosing round than in hunting. Sometimes a group of cats seemed to gather at the mill, prowling and yowling around the buildings, and the milk-white one was always there at the heart of the gathering. The miller's family began to feel uneasy about these goings-on. They set their boy, Giles, to watch over the buildings one such noisy night, with orders to strongly discourage the beasts.

This night, Giles surprised the cats in the barn and pounced. As they scattered, he flailed around with the knife he was holding, but only connected with one of the animals. He saw that he had cut off a paw, and picked it up, stroking its white fur. Of all the cats, he was glad that he had got this one; maybe now it would stay away - if it survived. And he lay down in the hay and dozed.

Come the morning, when he awoke, he

The shadow of Eagle Crag falls over the supposed graves of Lady Sibyl and Mother Helston

14

> *couldn't find the paw - for in its place was a human hand, with a wedding ring on its finger. He could guess the owner of this hand, and made his way to Bearnshaw Tower. When Lord William came to the door, Giles gave him the hand, wrapped in a strip of cotton.*
>
> *"I think, sir, I may have found something of her ladyship's" he said, and turned and left, his pockets jingling with what we might call 'hush money'.*
>
> *Lady Sybil was weak with loss of blood, but had enough energy to restore her hand to her wrist by the magic she had learned. She could not, however, take away the scar, and it is said that her descendants thereafter always had a strange birthmark around their wrist. Sybil certainly had the scar for the rest of her life, but that was not long, for after that dreadful night she never again recovered her full vigour. Within the year she was dead. Not surprisingly, perhaps, she was refused burial in consecrated ground and is said to have been buried at the foot of Eagle Crag, where she had loved to roam in her other forms; and where Mother Helston, dying soon after, was also buried.*
>
> *And it is said that if you walk under the Crag at around midnight on Hallowe'en, still you might see the white doe perched on the edge, held at bay by a horseman and an oddly-coloured dog.*

Fragments of this quite well-known tale have come to me orally from various sources, and reconstructions and investigations of the story have also appeared in print[1].

So look up at Eagle Crag if you're passing that way around Hallowe'en midnight, and you may see this old tale replayed. And who knows what else, at different times of the year? The Wild Hunt is also said to fly round the Crag on its route through the valley, both on Hallowe'en and at other times of the year. The Hunt is a pack of spectral dogs also known locally as the Gabriel Ratchets, who howl and yelp their way across the sky from Thieveley to Stoodley Pike, where they disappear into the earth[2]. To see them is an omen of misfortune, so don't be too eager! In 1665, Oliver Heywood wrote "there is also a strange noyse in the aire heard of many in these parts in this winter, called Gabriel-Ratches by this country people, the noyse is as if a great number of whelps were barking and howling, and tis observed that if any see them the persons that see them dye shortly after, they are never heard but before a great death or dearth"[3].

As for the transforming paw, this is a familiar motif in witch tales; Pennethorne Hughes[4] reports a hunter in Auvergne in the 16th century being set upon by a monstrous wolf. He managed to chop off a paw and escape with it, but at home he discovered in his pocket a hand with a wedding ring attached. He showed it to a friend, who recognised the ring as his wife's. She was found sitting by the fire at home, with an apron wrapped around her forearm.

Eagle Crag has also been known as Bill-Knipe, a name for which I have no explanation, and the Witches' Mounting Block, which is more understandable. There was a report in the *Todmorden and Hebden Bridge Historical Almanac* of 1882[5] that the crag was in danger of slipping downhill - thankfully that seems to have been a false alarm!

Another reputed witch, Loynd Wife, allegedly a confederate of the Pendle witches, was said to have used the crag as a look-out to spot victims, but the testimony against her, made by Giles Robinson in 1630, was thrown out as false witness. Robinson had claimed that he saw her on the Crag, and a wild storm blew up, during which a large black cat came to him and said "you cursed my mistress two days ago - she'll meet you in two days at Malkin Tower"; the cat then jumped up to the

The Old Woman at Portsmouth

rock - quite a distance and height from the road - and on to the woman's shoulder, before the two of them flew away. Robinson's son, Edmund, claimed in 1633 to have been at their gatherings, and gained local renown as a witch-finder, presumably with such tales as his father's. Seventeen people were found guilty of witchcraft through his evidence, four of whom were further examined by King Charles I in London. The upshot of this was that none of these was executed - though some died in prison, the last was released in 1636, and the Robinsons, when examined themselves, admitted perjury[6].

In Portsmouth, opposite the Roebuck Inn, a lane leads off up towards the moors. A little way up the lane is The Old Woman, a protruding cliff in the side of the valley. When you look at it from the main road, coming from Burnley, you can see why it's called that - it displays a simulacrum of the head and torso of an old woman with her hair set in a bun, almost a story-book witch. Her visibility depends on season and light, so don't be disappointed if you don't see her first time. Her name and appearance recalls the figure known in Gaelic lore as the 'Cailleach', traditionally the guardian of wild beasts like the deer and wolf, and in some Irish legends portrayed as a wealthy farmer; she has been associated with the Celtic goddess Anu or Danu. In Northern England, the equivalent figure in legend and place-name is 'the old woman' or 'the old wife'. There are obviously grounds for associating The Old Woman and the Cliviger witch tales with this ancient legendary figure[7].

A little further still up that lane you come to Bearnshaw Tower, Lady Sybil's home. The Tower used to stand at one end of the house, but according to Winnie Marshall[8] fell down in 1860 after attempts to find the rumoured treasure beneath it. Could this treasure have been lead, which was optimistically thought in the 17-18th centuries to be plentiful in the area? In 1627, Robert Hartley, a farmer at Thieveley, near Holme Chapel, dug a ditch near Dean Scout and found a vein of galena. This chance find became the Thieveley Lead Mine, and when the price of lead was high it looked sufficiently likely to be prosperous that it was commandeered in 1630 by King Charles I. In fact, it flopped and everybody concerned lost money until it was closed in 1635. Two further attempts at mining lead here were made in the eighteenth century, but were also abandoned[9].

The acquisitiveness of the Towneley family in the past[10] may account for their inclusion in this tale, as Anne Hewland[11] was unable to find any documentary evidence of a William Towneley (though she makes the point that the 'fulsome' Roby was "careful to state that Lord William was a 'connection' of the Towneley family", i.e. not a direct member). Nor was she able to find any evidence for a solitary heiress at Bearnshaw Tower, which belonged to the Lomax family before it was sold to - guess who - the Towneleys.

The two rock images of the Eagle and the Old Woman frame this tale of border witchcraft firmly within its local landscape.

1. See for example Hewland, who turns in a good historical investigation of the background to the tale; Holden; Topa, who reduces to a more palatable length and form Roby's long and melodramatic fictionalisation, which seems to be the earliest written source of the story; and an anonymous condensed version of Roby's account, which takes up six pages of small type in the *Todmorden and Hebden Bridge Historical Almanack* of 1877.
2. Harland & Wilkinson: 88-9; Whitaker
3. Heywood: 91
4. Hughes: 158
5. p.63
6. Hird; Thornber: 66
7. Grinsell; Jones; Taylor
9. Marshall: 25
9. Thornber: 60ff, 84
10. Thornber 1987: 42-44
11. Hewland: 7ff

Grinsell, Leslie. *The Folklore of Prehistoric Sites in Britain*. David & Charles, 1976, p.43-4
Harland, John & Wilkinson, T T. *Lancashire Folk-Lore*. 1882, repub EP, Leeds, 1973
Hewland, Anne P. 'In Search of Sybil', *Northern Earth* 67. 1996, pp.7ff

Heywood, Rev. Oliver. (Ed J Horsfall Turner). *Oliver Heywood 1630-1702: His autobiography, diaries, anecdote and event books, Vol. 3*. Brighouse, 1882
Hird, Frank. *Lancashire Stories*, Vol. 2
Holden, Joshua, *A Short History of Todmorden*. Manchester University Press, 1912
Hughes, Pennethorne. *Witchcraft*. Pelican, 1965
Jones, Alison. *Larousse Dictionary of World Folklore*. Larousse, 1996, p.88
Marshall, Winnie. *Cornholme, a Border Village*. priv. pub., 1984
Readers Digest. *Folklore, Myths & Legends of Britain*. 1973. p.362
Roby, John. *Traditions of Lancashire*. 1824, repub. Routledge, 1867
Taylor, Ian. 'Bride & the Old Wife'. *Northern Earth* 53 & 54, 1993
Thornber, Titus. *A Pennine Parish: the history of Cliviger*. Rieve Edge Press, Burnley, 1987
Todmorden and Hebden Bridge Historical Almanack 1877, pp.97-107; 1882
Topa, Caroline. 'A Ghostly Tale of Witchcraft and Mysterious Death', *Hebden Bridge Times*, April 27, 1979
Whitaker, Terence W. *Yorkshire's Ghosts & Legends*. Granada, 1983

2.

THE CLIVIGER BOGGART

All over the country, people have had to live with various kinds of 'little people', and tales were told of where they might be encountered. Generally it was not an encounter that you would seek, if you wanted a quiet life, since, while these beings could be helpful, there was usually a high likelihood of some mischief. In the Calder valley, the most common 'faerie' denizen is the boggart, and stories and rumours of them abound. Here is a tale that demonstrates a cheeky boggart's loyalty.

You never quite know where you are with boggarts. Sometimes they can be helpful little creatures around the house, but more often than not they're cussed little things that like to play tricks on people, especially when you find a boggart that likes to live outdoors. There are some folk, though, who have had reason to thank a boggart that for some good reason of its own has attached itself to them, for then much of the house and farm work gets done overnight, at a tremendous rate, and the people prosper well. But though they may have reason to thank the boggart, that is the one thing they shouldn't do, because either their little friend will storm off in a huff, and their work will never go so easy again, or the one who once helped them will turn to making mischief for them.

That was how it happened at a farm up on the Cliviger hillside when a new family moved in. A boggart took a particular liking to this family, and decided to share their house. Oh, odd jobs he'd do for them, but mostly he just played. Well, he called it play, but the family called it a plague, as beds jumped about and bedclothes were pulled off the sleeping children and crockery was moved from shelf to dresser and strange noises frightened them and their children at all hours of the day and night. No harm ever came to

> them, but it was a real trial. They asked the boggart to leave them alone, they asked him to be more careful, they thanked him for the work he'd done - but whatever they did or said the mischief continued. The boggart wasn't for turning. It wasn't very long before the whole family got so run down with the tricks that they reluctantly decided to move house and find somewhere else to farm in peace.
> So they boxed up their goods and loaded the boxes and their furniture on to a cart, and sadly they left the house they had hoped to make a living in. On the lane they saw a neighbour, who looked at them and at the laden cart in surprise.
> "Well, Will, what's all this about then?" he asked.
> "Ah, see, Tom, this place is no good for us. We're flittin'" replied Bill, looking sadly at his wife and children on the cart seat beside him, and they all nodded.
> "Flittin', tha say!"
> "Aye, that's reet, we're flittin'" piped up a strange high voice from among the boxes and chairs at the back of the cart. The whole family jumped and looked back at their heap of belongings. For a few moments nobody said anything. Then Will shrugged, and jerked the reins round.
> "Well" he said "if tha's flittin' too, we may as well flit back again".
> And the whole family, boggart and all, turned round and went back to their farm.

This story is an old chestnut in boggart lore, and by no means unique to this vicinity[1]. Indeed, versions have been recorded from all over the North, and even Lincolnshire and Shropshire, proving the popularity of a humorous yarn and its tendency to migrate wherever there's a tale to be told, at least at first glance. A 19th-century newspaper report provided the necessary credentials for the tale to be included in this local collection by placing the episode in Cliviger; which, whether in Lancashire or Yorkshire, Burnley or Calderdale, is still in my book in the upper Calder valley. Perhaps, however, there may be some truth in the tale, as Harland and Wilkinson reported meeting a young boy in Holme Chapel, who told them that "the boggart has driven William Clarke out of his house; he flitted last Friday", but in that case the house had remained empty - the boy invited them to see it, on Brown Hills in Burnley Wood.

The Cliviger valley, particularly nearer Burnley, was rich in lore and belief in supernatural visitants at the end of the 19th century. Indeed, this stretch of valley on the borders of Yorkshire and Lancashire seems to have been key fairy territory. A doggerel poet from Saddleworth noted that fairies were living there until "*the steeple rose / and bells began to play*" - at which point their Queen left for a wilder place, "*where Todmore's kingdom lay*"[2].

An older inhabitant of Worsthorne reaffirmed this belief, writing of 'brownies' being numerous at Brownside, hence the name. The ford, the kind of water site so often found in folklore dealing with liminal beings like fairies, was a favourite haunt of theirs, and a woman had once seen a naked brownie sitting behind a hedge there after midnight. This was none of the 'little people', but the size of a man. Today, more cynical as well as more sceptical, we might cast even more doubt than usual on the identification of this figure as a brownie, but neither the woman, identified by name in the article, nor the writer apparently doubted the attribution, and the description recurs in boggart lore. The writer mentioned other fairy haunts in the area, too - at Rowley, between the wood and the River Brun, where tiny clay pipes and scraps of tiny dresses had been found, and a boggart had been 'laid' (to halt a boggart's mischief, temporarily or permanently, is to 'lay' a boggart) at another water-site at Netherwood Bridge, where two streams joined at Water Meetings - a headstone was placed at the site to underscore the exorcism[3]. Nearby Extwhistle had more such experiences - a woman at High Halstead was concerned to find something in her cradle looking "as false as a boggart", but convinced the fairy kidnapper to return her baby when she started mistreating the changeling; and a local poacher bagged what he thought was a rabbit near the Hagg, but dropped his sack and ran when a high voice began calling out from it, and was answered by another nearby[4].

We also hear from this area of the Lubber Fiend, a local 'lob' - something akin to the boggart in that it likes certain households and is prepared to help out around the place in return for a bowl of milk and a seat by the fireside, but is distinct in that it is very large and hairy, with a long thin tail[5]. John Milton wrote in his 'L'Allegro' of this 'drudging Goblin', who, after doing his night's work, "stretch'd all out the Chimney's length / basks at the fire his hairy Strength". Lewis Spence has suggested that boggarts and suchlike who demonstrate a loyalty to a particular family are ancestral spirits.

Another Yorkshire favourite, the hob, makes its appearance in local lore, too, at Hob Hole Cottage, on the Barcroft estate and Hob Lane End near the Queen Hotel[6].

Boggarts are a variety of the so-called 'little people', but note that according to many traditional tales, including the Brownside encounter above, fairy kin are not necessarily much, if any, smaller than humans, and only seemed to shrink in stature - and dignity - under the influence of Victorian sensibilities. Boggarts seem to resemble brownies when visual contact has been reported, and share with brownies their mischievous (rather than malicious) character; but not everything that's called a boggart may be so, as the word was used typically in the past to describe a wide range of inexplicable and fearful experiences. What today we might refer to as a ghost or a poltergeist was frequently lumped in with boggarts; but who are we to tell? Perhaps the old tales know better than us, and hauntings actually are caused by boggarts!

Along with the Eagle Crag tale, with its witch and the Wild Hunt, this is a *very* strange valley indeed, and this is just a small part of our area! Place-names, such as the Boggart Stones above Gorple, indicate the local abundance of boggarts and their ilk all over Calderdale and surrounding districts, and surely we have not heard the last of them - even in this book!

1. Other versions of this story can be found in Gee, Briggs and other collections of fairy lore.
2. Bowker
3. *Todmorden and Hebden Bridge Almanac* 1883
4. Wilkinson & Tattersall: 61-2, 65
5. Harland & Wilkinson: 88-9; Franklin: 162
6. Thornber: 64, 153

Bowker, James. *Goblin Tales of Lancashire*. Sonnenschein, London 1893

Briggs, Katharine. *Abbey Lubbers, Banshees & Boggarts*. Kestrel, 1979

" ". *A Dictionary of Fairies*. Penguin, 1976

Franklin, Anna *The Illustrated Encyclopaedia of Fairies*. Vega 2002

Gee, H L. *Folk Tales of Yorkshire*. Thomas Nelson & Sons, 1952. 'The Farndale Hob'

Harland, John, & Wilkinson, T Tattersall. *Lancashire Folk-Lore*. 1882, repub EP 1973, p.61

Harte, Jeremy. *Exploring Fairy Traditions*. Heart of Albion, 2004

Simpson, J, & Roud, S. *Dictionary of English Folklore*. Oxford, 2000

Thornber, Titus. *A Pennine Parish: The History of Cliviger*. Rieve Edge, Burnley, 1987

Todmorden & Hebden Bridge Historical Almanac 1883

Wilkinson, T T. 'The Old Traditions & Customs of Lancashire', talk at Todmorden Mechanics Institution, 21 December, 1863; reported in *Todmorden Times* 26 December 1863

Wilkinson, T T & Tattersall, J F. *Memories of Hurstwood*, Lupton, 1889.

3.
THE BRIDE STONES

Towards the western end of the Calder Valley, at a height of some 1430 ft, a ridge of gritstone pushes out like a wave ready to break over Todmorden. Of all the outcrops in the valley, this is the one most weathered into fantastic shapes, strung out on two levels along a stretch of hillside half a mile long. Perhaps you'll see the sphinx, or the tortoise, or the whelk shell, or some other image that comes to mind in the motley creations of wind and rain.

On a more mundane level, at the western end are two sets of huge paired oblong rocks, about fifteen feet apart and parallel, with holes cut into them that indicate that once somebody's home was built between the two blocks.

The Bridestones have a rare numinous quality that enthuses the spirit and lends the mind to notions of magical presence - though this seems largely lost on the climbers who scramble over them. For many, the focus of the Bridestones' numen is the weird pillar at the eastern end of the ridge. It is around fifteen feet tall and shaped like an upturned bottle, balanced on its neck; though as this is the rock known as the Bride, we should rather see the neck of the bottle as the Bride's slender waist. Beside it is a smaller chunk of stone, also slightly rounded, laying on the ground. This is a stone once known as the Groom, and between them there is a tale to tell.

Some say that the Bridestones were where the first marriage took place in the district, which may say more about old Todmorden than about the antiquity of the tale. Indeed, the stones witnessed the first meeting of the future couple, who went by the names of Nan Moor and Jack Stone. Nan was already living among the stones, in a house built roughly among the stones, and this provided a fine shelter for the lovers to get better acquainted.

In a short time, as they were getting on so well together, they felt they wanted to make their association more permanent and hit on the idea of plighting their troth between the two strange pillars at the eastern end of the stones. They declared their love would remain steadfast through thick and thin, just like the two rocks with their massive girths and narrow pedestals; and satisfied with the symbolism of the idea, they called their friends together and held a little ceremony there, with the Bride on one side and the Groom on the other. Then they went back to their hut, home now to the married couple.

Life passed happily enough for a while, but Jack's work took him out and about the area. Sometimes, naturally, he would be invited by his employer to sup with them, and sometimes he would drop in at the inn on his way home. Often it would be late when Jack got back to his house among the stones. She was not best pleased, and told him so. The more it happened, the more Nan complained, and of course the more she complained, the more Jack felt nagged and aggrieved.

One night, after another of their increasingly common rows, Jack stormed out of the hut in a rage, and off he went back to his old haunts in the valley. If it really was the first marriage, then it seemed likely to be heading for the first divorce as well.

Jack sorely rued the day he got wed, and he sorely rued the fact that he got wed at all, and he rued even more the whole business of marriage and coupledom. He no longer had fond memories of the rocks where they had met, and where they had enjoyed many happy hours before and after their wedding vows. Instead, he began to feel that it was those rocks, with their damnable 'thick and thin' symbolism, that had been his downfall, and that he,

Jack Stone, would be their downfall. He declared to his friends that the stones would never again trick a man into marriage if he had anything to do with it and on one particularly thirsty occasion he fired them all up to join him on a job he had lined up at the Bridestones. "Go get your mattocks and picks" he said, "you'll need 'em".

So off they trudged up the hill, with their tools over their shoulders or helping them climb up the slope. In time they arrived at the stones, and Jack made straight for the Bride and Groom. He swung his pick at the narrow waist of the Groom, and all joined in lustily.

Under the barrage of blows, it wasn't long before a loud cracking sound was heard; the men jumped back, and the great stone groaned and toppled to the ground, where it lies now. The men cheered, and turned then to the taller Bride; but something made them hold back. It was Jack who moved first; he who had launched the attack on the Groom stepped forward, raised his pick back over his shoulder, and swung it at the Bride's waist. The weapon crashed into the rock surface, and just as the iron hit the stone, an unearthly cry, something between a scream and a howl, echoed around the stones.

Not another pick, not another mattock swung that day, as Jack and all his mates dropped their tools and high-tailed it back to town. No doubt they steadied their frayed nerves with a top-up drink before they began to review and retell events, as much for the benefit of themselves as for their neighbours.

There were some people who heard their tale who said the scream was probably Nan, hiding among the rocks. After all, she still lived in the hut she and Jack had shared. But Jack and his friends were not convinced. They were there, they'd heard the cry, and for them, it was the Bride herself that had warned them off.

The notion of the Bridestones as an early marriage venue is common locally, but I collected the more complete version of the story from the 1887 edition of the *Todmorden and Hebden Bridge Historical Almanac*, where it appears to be a concoction of legend and Victorian embroidery, and placed "sometime before the middle of the last [i.e. eighteenth] century". At that time, said the article, the marks of Jack's pick were still visible. I've tried not to put any twenty-first-century embroidery on it, though the frills are definitely contemporary[1].

The Bridestones are first mentioned in local documents in 1491, and Smith, in his 'Placenames of the West Riding', does not quibble with the derivation from 'bryd', a bride. Watson attempts to reconstruct a Druidical wedding ceremony at the spot: "a stone pillar, amongst people who dealt so much in representations, was no unfit emblem of the strong and perpetual obligation the contracting parties laid themselves under" - hence Jack's sense of oppression, perhaps. John Stansfeld, however, in 1885, suggested that Danish 'bred' and Icelandic 'bryddr' married well with Gaelic 'braidh' and modern 'bride' in meaning 'edge of the top of the hill'; whether today's etymologists feel this explanation is defensible or not, the descriptive does fit this location rather well.

There is to my mind an implication in the story that Nan Moor was a kind of guardian of the Bridestones - she did, after all, choose to live there, and there she met Jack, and some suspect her of being the origin of the terrible cry and she continued to live there even after the desecration of the stones. Taylor has suggested an identification of Bride with 'the Old Wife' or Gaelic Cailleach, a traditional spiritual denizen of wild places more usually associated with the Irish goddess Danu; a local appearance of this hag figure may well be the Old Woman (see 'The Witch of Eagle Crag').

The whole ridge is known as the Bridestones. It has been said that placenames like this refer to the pre-Christian British goddess Bride, perhaps also known as Brigit or Brigantia. The last-named was a goddess of high places who was also the tutelary goddess of the Brigantes, the tribal federation covering much of northern England when the Romans arrived. The Bridestones would be an appropriate shrine for such a dizzy deity. There was also a Christian St Bride, commonly found in church dedications in Cumbria and the Isle of Man, whom many think to be a Christianisation of the ancient goddess. However, more recent place-name research has suggested caution is required in attributing Bride placenames to the goddess, as well as St Bride to the Iron Age goddess, and of course there is Stansfeld's suggestion above; so we must regard the claim to ancient dedication to Bride/Brigit as unproven.

There is another 'Bride' place-name in the upper Calder valley, incidentally in a location that would accord with Stansfield's etymology; Bridewell Head spring is mentioned on an 1820 gravestone in Crimsworth Cemetery, Pecket Well, but by 1900 it had become known as Brigwell Head (which may suggest that the original pronunciation of this 'bride' was 'brid').

I have a whimsy that once came to me while I was among the rocks - that the Bridestones, which stand at the hub of and overlooking three valleys, can be imagined to symbolise the union of the three peoples who founded the modern settlements of the valley - the British, whose presence is remembered in the 'wal' (i.e. Welsh) placenames like Walsden in the southern valley leading from Littleborough; the Norse, who would have come into the valley from their Lancashire holdings via the northern valley from Burnley; and the English, who named most of the valley to the east.

The rock-house at Fast Ends

The Bride has also been known locally as the Bottle Neck. Other rocks have been given names, too, arising from one perception or another. Modern climbers have named rocks themselves, like the Indian's Head and Spy Hole Pinnacle, as well as giving equally vivid names, like the Obscene Cleft, to specific routes[2]. F A Leyland cites names known in the nineteenth century, like Table Rock and Toad Rock.

The formation known to climbers as Big Sister and Little Brother - "two upright slabs of millstone grit, of colossal size, some 19' apart, between which a two-storey house was formerly built, but long since removed", is where Nan and Jack, in the legend, made their home. This was once known, suitably enough, as Fast-Ends - "The cottage was a most remarkable structure, two of its sides being formed of solid rock (hence its name), and a portion of the third side being also a large rock. These, with cupboards cut out of them with the chisel, still remain... with the exception of the above traces of a rude pantry, there is no evidence of the place ever having been tenanted by man. But tenanted it was, and for some years, by the Stansfield family"[3]. This was at some period between 1802 and 1820. Perhaps unsurprisingly given the situation of this cottage, one of those tenants, Abraham Stansfield, became a noted naturalist.

John Watson knew of the Bride and Groom in 1789, but does not give details of the legend, other than saying the Groom had been "thrown down by the country people". In keeping with the spirit of his time, however, he saw the rocks as the natural haunt of "a large settlement" of Druids - "a vast variety of rocks and stones so scattered about the common, that at first view the whole looked something like a temple of the serpentine kind".

The writer of an 1887 article[4] wonders aloud what the Bridestone might say if she were able to speak, and suggests she might say "It pities the heart of a stone to see the indifference of mankind". Well might he have suggested this, for despite the Bride being without doubt a local wonder, sad to say is now under pressure from climbers. Pick-marks are still as visible as in 1887, but now they are not the work of old Jack, but of modern climbers. Apart from general damage to the protective natural patina of the rock surface, ledges have been pecked out of the grit for footholds, while feet scrabbling for a hold have further been wearing away the waist, which now appears to be cracked; reports have come in that the Bride rocks slightly, suggesting that the crack is serious enough that the stone might fall if such pressure continues. Local climbers' associations and other organisations have urged their members not to attempt this rock, but the damage is continuing, and other measures would seem to be needed to keep climbers off the Bride - they might yet do what Jack Stone failed to achieve, and who would hear the scream then?

Edward Wilms' sketch of the Bridestones in the 19th-century (in Leyland)

1. See also Grinsell: 175; Smith: 174
2. Musgrove: 86-101
3. *Todmorden & Hebden Bridge Historical Almanac*, 1882
4. *Todmorden & Hebden Bridge Historical Almanac*, 1887

Billingsley, John. 'The Bride Before A Fall', *Peak & Pennine*. June 1998
Grinsell, Leslie V. *The Folklore of Prehistoric Sites in Britain*. David & Charles, 1976, p.175
Haigh, Mike. 'The Cumbrian Bride Church Cluster', *Northern Earth* 57, 1994
Leyland, F A. *The History & Antiquities of the Parish of Halifax, by the Rev. John Watson, with additions and corrections*. Leyland & Son, Halifax, & Longmans, London, n.d.
Musgrove, Dave. *Yorkshire Gritstone*. Yorkshire Mountaineering Club, 1998
Smith, A H. *The Place Names of the West Riding of Yorkshire Pt III*. Cambridge University Press, 1961, p.174
Stansfeld, John. *The History of the Family of Stansfeld of Stansfield*. Goodall & Suddick, Leeds, 1885
Taylor, Ian. 'Bride & the Old Wife'. *Northern Earth* 53 & 54, 1993
Todmorden and Hebden Bridge Historical Almanac 1884, p.13; 1887, 'The Township of Stansfield' pp.129-137
Watson, John. *The History & Antiquities of the Town & Parish of Halifax*. J Milner, Halifax, 1789, p.15

4.
THE EVE STONE

I do not actually know which is the Eve Stone that is referred to in this story, as it does not appear on maps and was unknown to the local people I have asked. However, the story is quite specific about its location on Langfield Common, near the road out of Lumbutts, towards the Shepherds Rest pub, and there are several potential candidates for the Eve Stone on the moors side of the lane. It is possible, I think, that the name should be spelt Eaves Stone, in line with the local term for precipitous edges like the one standing above the common.

This is a real fairy story.

> We all know them, don't we? Those people who are ready to lift something that's not theirs and then swear blind they're innocent.
>
> There was a man in Walsden had a real name for that. Rob o'Harry'o't'Deans was what he was generally known by - to his face, at any rate. People called him something else behind his back, as anything left outside on the street for more than a minute or two, it was gone, and there was Rob, tut-tutting and shaking his head, full of sympathy and saying he reckoned it must be the fairies, the way things just disappeared, with no one seeing. And no one could catch him in the act, but if anyone made a pointed comment, he acted all injured.
>
> So Rob, though he could tell a good story and was entertaining enough at the inn, wasn't a very popular man in the village, and the fairies, when they heard what he'd been saying, weren't too pleased, either. The little folk kept themselves to themselves and weren't usually very interested in folks' doings – and folk were happy enough to leave things like that, and not tempt their tempers. But it irked them to be spoken ill of, particularly for none of their doing. They couldn't do any more to Rob than the village could - but they kept an eye on him all the same.

Rob liked a drink, and if he could have a drink and pay for it after with a bit of thieving, that was a good night for him. He used to go round and visit inns here and there, and there was one night he came over to Mankinholes, and supped quite late there. It was well dark and quiet when he set off home, and he didn't disturb the villagers as he found his way into one of their warehouses and came out with a couple of pieces of worsted. He didn't go by the road home, though, of course - he kept to the moor edge. And that's when the fairies saw their chance.

Near Croft he came on to the causey that'd take him back over the moor to Walsden. But as he was coming up to the big rock there, the one called Eve Stone, he heard a noise ahead, and quickly ducked behind the stone. What he heard sounded something like a bit of a do - laughing and giggling and a bit of a crash of crockery, and some fine music to go with it, too. Amazed, Rob also got curious. Carefully, he removed his clogs, so he wouldn't make any noise, and inched himself up to the top of the stone.

What he saw was a feast, like a celebration, with a long table set up with a lantern on a pole at its centre; and covered with cups and dishes, and little people all around it, dressed to the nines. To one side, as he watched, an old man played with tiny children, blowing great big bubbles from a pan, and the children chased them, laughing, as the bubbles floated up and away towards the moor - straight towards the stone where Rob was lying, in fact, and some of them burst against the rock and spattered into Rob's face. It was a job to keep from sneezing and giving himself away, to be sure. Well, the fairies looked set up for the night, and Rob began to get sleepy - after all, he thought, he'd had a lot to drink that night, and the fairies would surely be off before light, and he could get on home safely then. Maybe they might even leave some of their fine-looking cutlery or crockery for him to pick up. Fairy stuff would fetch a good price... And with this comfortable thought, he laid his head on his arm and went to sleep.

Well, of course, the little folk already knew all about him there behind the rock. As soon as they were sure that their bubbles had sent him to sleep, the old man clapped his hands and several of the

> *younger ones scurried around behind the Eve Stone. They had no fear of waking Rob - they knew he'd be asleep till the morning was properly come. And they put the clogs back on his feet, and they laid one piece of worsted under his head for a pillow, and the other under his arm, and as the first light began to show they all ran off, well pleased with themselves.*
>
> *People were up and about early in those days, and it wasn't long before someone saw Rob sleeping there, and got suspicious about the worsted packs. So they went off and called in the local constable, and when Rob awoke, it was with some very stern-looking faces around him.*
>
> *Nobody heard the fairies laugh, as he was arrested and taken off to Halifax. And that's the last anyone in the area saw of Rob - whether he went to the Gibbet or scaffold, or ended his days in York Prison, I don't know, but surely he'd be remembering that night at the fairy feast until his last moments.*

This tale I have only come across once, and that in written form, in the *Todmorden and Hebden Bridge Historical Almanack*, p.60-61, where it was attributed to a certain 'Aunt Susey'[1].

---

1. *Todmorden & Hebden Bridge Historical Almanac*, 1874: 60-61

Thanks go to Paul Degnan for putting me on to this story.

5.
STOODLEY PIKE

Stoodley Pike, featured in the cover photo, is perhaps the most prominent landmark of the valley, the tapering pinnacle of the monument rising from a tongue of moorland poking out into the centre of the valley. Even the river detours to avoid it; or is it just to make the most of the view from the valley? The name predates the present monument and is even mentioned on Carey's 1794 map of England. 'Pike' is a name often given to a cairn or mound, and there is a strong likelihood that there was a prehistoric cairn, perhaps a burial mound, on the spot.

So Stoodley Pike has been a place of some significance for a long time, and over time has collected rumours and legends that all tend to characterise it as a rather strange place...

Nobody really knows whether they like it, that spike on top of the hill over there, but they all agree that, like it or not, there's been something there since way back. They found bones there, you know, when they were clearing a pile of stones to make the first tower, but they still built it. Maybe the bones were of some chief way back when, or maybe it was true what some people said, that there was a murder up there. Not sure whether it was right to build on someone's grave like that, but some people used to say bones make a good foundation. Anyway, I suppose some reverent words were said by somebody. I would hope so, anyway, but you don't know, do you?

There was something odd that happened when the masons laid the foundation stone, though. They used a sword, you know, and apparently a little boy, sat on his dad's shoulders, got a bit too close to the action, and the sword cut him as it was being swung round. One fellow told me it was half-deliberate, as this lad kept leaning in closer and closer and wouldn't be told, and nor would his dad. So there. Well, whatever, the lad wasn't badly hurt, mostly shocked, but a quantity of blood got spilt. It's one thing building on bones, but in the old days they reckoned mortar was stronger if mixed with blood, and you need a bit of strength if you're going to build something up there.

But it didn't work so well, anyway. They built it in 1814 - well, it was 1815 before they finished it, just after the Battle of Waterloo. And forty years later, down it all came in a great clatter of stone.

Perhaps they should have taken better care of those bones, or the boy, or maybe it was for another reason it fell down. Everybody round here thought so. You see, that monument was put up to celebrate peace against Napoleon, peace, rather than a war memorial. Which is a grand gesture, even if some cynical folk did point out that it was a bit rich the clothiers around here contributing to a peace monument, since they'd been supplying uniforms to all armies on both sides in the war, and the more blood was spilt, the more uniforms they sold. There were men that made their fortunes out of the war, right enough, and so some say the new Pike was a kind of sop for their consciences.

Be that as it may, it was there as a peace monument and that made it all the stranger when it fell down in 1854, because it fell down on the day that the Russian ambassador left London, and the next day, we were in the Crimean War. They said the cement had weakened in the joints, after being struck by lightning a few years before, but in the end it seemed that that peace monument took itself very seriously.

Well, it was rebuilt two years later and made a lot stronger this time, and we've had no end of wars since then. Mind you, it's still a funny sort of place. There were stories told before they built those towers, that the Devil lived up there, or underneath there, rather, and if a stone was dislodged from the old cairn, a great flame would spring up from below and none of the local farms would get any rest until someone went up from Stoodley, it had to be them, to replace it. And sometimes the Old Fellow would have some kind of party with his imps and demons, and things would just go wrong in the area - milk would go sour, or cream wouldn't churn, or cows went sick or mad with the 'turn i'th'yead', as they called it.

They still say sometimes you can see lights shining out from the hillside up there, even though they've built on the old cairn; and that it means some kind of gate is open up there, open that is in the hillside, through to another world - whether it's the Devil's place or the fairies' abode no one seems quite sure. It's supposed to be foggy nights that it's most likely to open. Some people say these strange lights are UFOs, and the Todmorden area is supposed to be a real hot spot for UFOs, or at least for strange lights in the sky. And as for the Devil, I reckon it's a great place for him, too, and they do say he stepped across from Stoodley Pike to the Devil's Rock, over the valley by Blackshaw, but that's another story.

The first of the latter-day memorials on Stoodley Pike was begun in 1814 to commemorate the surrender of Paris; work was suspended after Napoleon left his agreed exile on Elba, re-igniting the conflict, and finished after Waterloo. Its collapse in a storm on February 8, 1854, the same afternoon that the Russian ambassador left London, signalling the outbreak of the Crimean War, could not have failed to be ominous - and to confirm the rather spooky reputation that the place obviously held in local tradition.

The cause of the collapse was ascribed to the effects of the elements, not least a lightning strike some years before its collapse, but any similar structural problems were mostly rectified in the 1856-58 reconstruction (restoration was needed in 1889, when a lightning conductor was also installed) that we see today. The belief that cement mixed with blood - especially human blood - is stronger than standard mortar is familiar in the folklore record and is usually taken as an echo of ancient foundation sacrifices and offerings. The experience of the young boy at the 1814 foundation ceremony, who was sitting and squirming on his father's shoulders, and from whose head "blood flowed freely" when cut by the Tyler's sword, is a curiously potent coincidence, not rendered any less potent by the continuation of the proceedings, in which a whole sheep was roasted and shared!

A similar story to the Pike's ominous collapse is told of the World War One memorial in Ripponden. Here, the bayonet on the soldier's rifle suddenly snapped at the outbreak of World War Two.

The cynicism which some have felt over the financing of the peace monument - the major part of the cost was subscribed by local textile manufacturers who had made considerable sums in supplying uniforms to all sides in the long war - was not shared by Tony Heginbottom, who argued for the sincerity of the local desire for peace and emphasised the active involvement of local Quakers, who were relatively numerous in Langfield, in its planning:

The Pike, seen from near Stoodley

"Throughout the war dissenters had occupied the moral high ground. In peacetime their monument continued to do so in physical and symbolic terms"[1]. Over the entrance was placed the inscription, 'This monument was erected by public subscription, to commemorate the peace, Anno Domini 1814'. Its pacifist symbolism was reaffirmed in 1962 and again in the 1970s when the CND symbol was daubed on its side.

The first monument stood just over 113 ft tall, and consisted of a square base with a cylinder, topped with a cone, above it; inside, over 156 steps led in an unrailed open spiral to a room and fireplace at the top of the cylinder. Vandalism led to the door being walled up. The present monument is 120 feet in height, with the gallery at the 40 ft mark, and at the time of construction it was probably the largest obelisk in the world.

Freemasons were certainly actively involved in planning the second monument, and their symbols remain in the architecture. Over the doorway can be seen a crossed compass and square and the six-pointed 'Star of David', whose interlocking triangles represent 'as above, so below'. There was no public event like the 1814 foundation ceremony, but doubtless a masonic rite was performed, and Heginbottom suggested that it may have been a rite of consecration. The chosen obelisk design surely conformed to masonic predilections (hence its use for the Washington Monument in America); originating in ancient Egypt, it was a sacred architectural form associated with the sun-god Ra, and later Osiris. Heginbottom remarked that the obelisk adds another layer of meaning to the peace monument - that of "a symbol of the Masonic God the Architect"[1]. We might also add that the obelisk form represents the *axis mundi*, or world axis, and note how the current monument does indeed seem to be a fixed point around which the Upper Calder valley revolves.

Steve Hanson has suggested that the design of the Pike, in particular the staircase to the balcony, which one accesses under the masonic signs over the doorway, further encodes masonic symbolism into the architecture: "the ascent in total darkness appears to replicate the masonic blindfold ceremony, a trial by ordeal, a leap of faith, after which enlightenment is received with the removal of the blindfold and acceptance into the order... the Pike might be designed to replicate this ceremony for the layperson: ascent by ordeal, followed by a privileged view..."[2]. The addition of a grill in the 1889 restoration only slightly diluted any such symbolism.

The flames which leapt from Stoodley Pike thirty years later were not the mysterious flares of folklore, but a beacon lit there to mark Queen Victoria's Golden Jubilee in 1887. At 1310 ft above sea level and so prominent as to be seen for miles around, it is unlikely that this was the only time the hilltop would have been used for a beacon fire.

The present obelisk, then, is a successor to the original peace monument of 1815, which itself was a successor to 'a rude heap of stones', probably a burial cairn, but reports vary. A writer in the *Todmorden and Hebden Bridge Historical Almanac*[3] claimed that a complete human skeleton was found while the foundations were being dug, but other writers have contested this. John Travis, who provided the source for the story of the flame shooting up from the cairn and the Devil's parties, wrote that some of the workmen felt that the bones were incomplete and not definitely human - they were black, and found at a great depth[4]. We might think, however, that these workmen may themselves have been influenced by the tales of imps dwelling below the Pike. Abraham Newell admitted that the bones were not definitely identified as human, but were found below a quantity of stones, and adds that "legends of the area lend colour to the view that the place was the site of a human burial or tragedy"[5], such as that rumoured in another local tale, that somebody had been murdered and buried there, more recently. These stories, of course, are not necessarily mutually exclusive.

Was there another monument on the site before the 1814 construction? H C Collins tells what I think is an unlikely tale, that "it was decided to erect a memorial on this site where an obelisk used to stand commemorating Austin Stoodley, an officer under Fairfax at Marsden [sic] Moor"[6]. However, I have not come across any other reference to such an early obelisk.

It is interesting that Travis gives a clear indication that it was the inhabitants of Stoodley - not Mankinholes or Lumbutts - who were responsible for the upkeep of the cairn, and that it was felt that misfortune would occur if the cairn was not properly cared for. Stoodley appears to have first appeared on record in the Wakefield Court Rolls of 1274. A similar tradition of cairn guardianship is recorded by Leyland for Sleepy Lowe, in Warley.

The episode where the young boy was injured by the Masons' sword is given in most popular accounts of the Pike. William Law commemorated the folklore of the Pike in verse in 1832. The story of a door opening in the hillside on foggy nights, and that the appearance of a strange light up there means the door is open, is one I heard told in the 1970s and 1990s; while the repute of Stoodley Pike and indeed the whole Todmorden area as a UFO hotspot is part of the valley's current folklore[7].

See the chapter on Great Rock for the story of the Devil's stride from Stoodley Pike to Blackshaw.

1. Heginbottom: 113-123
2. Hanson, *Todmorden News*.
3. *Todmorden and Hebden Bridge Historical Almanac*, 1890: 33-47
4. Travis: 14-15
5. Newell: 33-34
6. Collins, 27-28
7. See Randles, 1983, for this and a memorable local episode in Britain's UFO files - the abduction of PC Alan Godfrey in Todmorden.

Collins, H. C. *Rambles around Rochdale*. No date or publisher given.
Hanson, Steve. Letter, *Todmorden News*, Dec. 3, 2005
Heginbottom, J A. 'The Stoodley Pike Obelisk: a Commemorative Monument 1793-1889'. *Halifax Antiquarian Society Transactions* 1994, pp.113-123
Collins, H. C. *Rambles around Rochdale*. No date or publisher given.
Hanson, Steve. Letter, *Todmorden News*, Dec. 3, 2005
Heginbottom, J A. 'The Stoodley Pike Obelisk: a Commemorative Monument 1793-1889'. *Halifax Antiquarian Society Transactions* 1994, p.113-123
Law, William. 'Wanderings of a Wanderer'. Poem, 1832, excerpted in Savage, p.31
Leyland, F A. *The History & Antiquities of the Parish of Halifax, by the Rev. John Watson, with additions and corrections*. Leyland & Son, Halifax, & Longmans, London, n.d. p.51
Newell, Abraham. *A Hillside View of Industrial History*. Priv, Todmorden, 1925, p.33-4
Randles, Jenny. *The Pennine UFO Mystery*. Granada, 1983
Savage, E M. *Stoodley Pike*. Todmorden Antiquarian Society, 1974
Todmorden and Hebden Bridge Historical Almanac, 1867, p.27; 1890, p.33-47
Travis, John. *Round About Todmorden*. Chambers, Todmorden, 1890, p.14-15

6.
GREAT ROCK

Early 20th century postcard (courtesy Hebden Bridge Local History Society)

On a ledge of hillside below Staups Moor, in Blackshaw, a massive outcrop of millstone grit knuckles out from the ground. Its surface has been something of a canvas for the usual succession of sweethearts and tourists to etch their initials into the rock, but it is as a prominent landmark that it has obtained the legend that gives rise to another local name - Devil's Rock.

From here you can look clear across the valley to the pinnacle of Stoodley Pike, which also features in this tale, and whose stories were told in the previous chapter.

> There was a time, I hear, when God and the Devil got on really well, and they would go off on walkabout together, checking out the world and the people they found within it. For they were always finding new communities springing up in out of the way places, places that neither of them had known were inhabited or even in some cases inhabitable. The proof of human resourcefulness pleased God particularly, as he fancied he'd had something to do with bringing it about - but the Devil knew that the most he'd done was allow humans enough free will to make them cussed. But that's another story, better told elsewhere, and our tale tells of when these two met up at an ancient cairn that the Devil used to frequent, at the place we call Stoodley Pike. They cast an eye out over the view before them, and there, in a little meeting of three valleys,

like the grounds at the bottom of a cup, was Hebden Bridge. And it was new to them.

They watched the people in the streets below for a while, watched as they went about their daily business and watched as some of them got up to stranger antics, like catching rats with their teeth or putting larks in boxes and taking them to sing in pubs. It was when they saw men and women racing naked through the streets that the Devil said "Reckon this lot's mine".

Now, one of the less endearing habits of deities is to gamble with the fate of humans, and these two chancers played games to see which of them would get first option on the souls of any new communities they found. They didn't do it everywhere, just the places where people seemed to do things a bit differently, a bit unnecessarily - and Hebden Bridge wasn't that different then from what it is now. So God knew Lucifer's opening gambit well enough, and he rose to the occasion.

"You'll not get them that easy, Luce. You'll have to work for them, you know that. Hey now, see that great rock over there on the other side of the valley?" - and God pointed out the outcrop nearly two miles away. "If you can step from here to there in one stride, you can have them. If not, we'll give them a bit longer to make their minds up".

"You're on" said his companion, squinting across the valley. He set his right foot firmly on the edge of the hillside and stepped out with his left. He stretched, and as he stretched, he cast a shadow across the valley, which made people look up. Well, they groaned as they saw the Devil stretching out over the valley, because they'd heard of this kind of antic before, in other towns, and everybody agreed it was tiresome having your soul played for like this. So they watched, frowning, but not a little impressed, as the Devil reached further, and then still further, till he could look down and see the little river far below him in the middle of the valley, and the people looking up, and then he reached a bit further, until at last his foot came down with a hefty plonk on top of Great Rock. You can still see the imprint his hoof left on the rock, if you climb up on to the top.

Then came the tricky bit. The Devil was at full stretch, and he had to get his other leg across safely to win the game. He took a deep breath, and pulled his right leg after him - but he was stretched just that little bit too far, and as his weight shifted, he lost his grip on the top of Great Rock. His hoof scraped across the edge of the rock, and literally 'nicked' a chunk out of it; then that hoof came skittering down the front of the rock, leaving a big crack from top to bottom - and like the hole he left when he landed, you can still see that crack today, that's how hard he fell. And his hoof went scraping right down the side of the hill, and later they used the gouge for the track up from the valley. And fall he did, as he had done countless times before, in an ignominious heap at the foot of the valley, and if they hadn't built the railway and those mills at Eastwood I reckon you'd be able to see where he landed.

The Devil had lost his bet and God was laughing like a drain on Stoodley Pike; but the people watching reckoned that he'd made such a good effort that they'd give him a fair chance when it came to reckoning up at the end, and as I say, Hebden Bridge hasn't changed that much since then.

And we still call it Devil's Rock in memory of the time when the Old Man nearly had first claim on our souls. At least we have the choice now.

I have mostly come across this tale - which must I suppose be counted as one of the more apocryphal Legends of the Fall - in oral form, from numerous sources. I have also heard it, though much less often, in reverse, i.e. the Devil steps off from Great Rock across the valley to Stoodley Pike. In this version, the basin in the top of the rock is the imprint left by him grinding his hoof in for good grounding[1], and the nick in the edge of the basin and the crack down the rock face are the result of his back leg slipping as he reaches Stoodley Pike. Presumably in this version, too, it would be the Devil's hoof that laid down the route of the hillside track that approximately aligns between the two sites. Either way, he lost the wager! In the only early textual reference I have so far found, the Devil stepped off from Stoodley Pike[2].

A member of Mytholmroyd Historical Society, at a talk I gave there in December 2000, said he had heard that the Devil had taken several steps across the valley, the remains of which can still be seen. Perhaps the quarry by the railway at Cockden Hill is one, but I'm still looking - can anyone help?

It is of course a chicken-and-egg conundrum, but which came first, the name or the story? Was it called Devil's Rock from some

The bull engraving at Great Rock

piece of now-forgotten folklore? Or was the story created to explain away the basin at the top of the rock, and the dreadful fissure down its front? Though nothing can now be proven, I suspect the latter, and that the Devil (or at least strange and disturbing activity) was already associated with Stoodley Pike when this tale was created; and with the Pike being so directly in line of sight across the valley, from there, it's just a short step, as it were, to implicate the Devil in the Rock's appearance. And incidentally, the tale - at least the version that has him stepping off from Stoodley Pike - fulfils another traditional function of folklore, in talking up one's neighbourhood at the expense of another; because it suggests that the Devil couldn't get a foothold on the Stansfield/Blackshaw Head hillside. You can almost hear the storyteller adding "not like *some* places we could mention...".

Can we see God and Satan as buddies? Christian doctrine makes Satan the enemy of God, but there is a different interpretation of Satan's revolt and rejection in Islamic tradition. Here, Satan is God's greatest adherent, who stood by his primary vow, God's commandment to the angels to bow to none but himself. When God changed his tune and asked the angels to serve humanity, Satan felt unable to violate his first vow and put people between him and his love of God - in other words, he loved God too much; when he refused this edict, God sent him away, and in this interpretation, the anguish of Hell is the anguish of separation from the Beloved[3].

Aside from the initials and other graffiti of its countless visitors, the rock has attracted an artistic hand, too. A very minimalist etching of a running bull, in a style reminiscent of the Uffington White Horse in Dorset, can be found on a ledge among graffiti lettering, while up and around a corner, near the top of the Rock, is a similarly simple representation of a bull's head, with horns curved like a crescent above it[4]. There is no way of telling when these were made - the resemblance to the Uffington White Horse was commented on, spontaneously and uninvited, by prehistoric art specialist, Dr Masaru Ogawa, on a visit to the Rock, which is testimony to the timeless echo of the image; unfortunately, due to the local weather conditions that we know all too well and their exposed position, we must assume these carvings are not contemporary with the Iron Age hill figure they resemble.

Great Rock is rich in nomenclature - as well as its two popular names, it is probably also the Grisly Stone referred to by Leyland, without explanation.

In the story, I make reference to some folklore of the Hebden Bridge area. The man who caught rats with his teeth at Stubbing Wharf, Billy Red, appears in a short story by Ted Hughes[5]; larkmen would steal baby larks from their moorland nests, and train them as pet birds to sing in competitions[6], the Brig Races were an annual tradition, held in August, when men dressed in at most a loincloth, and women dressed only in a chemise, would run from the White Lion to Mayroyd and back for a prize - a new chemise for the women, but for the men a hat (perhaps strategically placed)[7]. Lark singing died out in the early twentieth century; the naked races about a century before that.

1. Included also in local testimony recorded by Bob Pegg, and broadcast in part as 'The Town in the Valley', BBC Radio Leeds, 1980s.
2. *Todmorden Herald* 2 May, 1906
3. Campbell: 255-6
4. Thanks to Jonathan Coe for pointing the bull out to me.
5. 'Sunday', *Wodwo*.
6. Pegg: 126-7; Horsfield.
7. Pegg: 126; 'Antiquarian'.

'Antiquarian', *Sketches of Old Hebden Bridge & its People*. Wm Ashworth & Son, HB, 1882. Repub. with illus. as *Old Hebden Bridge & its People* by Jack Uttley (ed), Mytholmroyd, 1990
Campbell, Joseph. *The Power of Myth*. Doubleday-Anchor, 1988
Horsfield, Margaret. 'Lark Ascending', *Milltown Memories* 4, Summer 2003, p.10
Leyland, F A. *The History & Antiquities of the Parish of Halifax, by the Rev. John Watson, with additions and corrections*. Leyland & Son, Halifax, & Longmans, London, n.d. p.47
Pegg, Bob. *Rites & Riots*. Blandford, 1981
Todmorden Herald 2 May, 1906

7.
TOM BELL'S CAVE

Calderdale is the right kind of area for outlaws, and it's had its share in history. Whether Tom Bell ever existed in fact is open to question, but there's a cave named after him in Hardcastle Crags, and need we more proof?

A real local character was a man called Bell, Tom Bell. He lived in a cave in the woods, in a terrible gorge choked with great fallen boulders and trees whose roots sneaked like snakes between the gaps in the rocks. At that time, Hardcastle Crags was just the right kind of place for an outlaw, and that's what he was.

He wasn't the proper robbing sort of outlaw, though, at least not that I've heard. He was no highwayman, holding people up at pistol point. He didn't have a robber band, either, although he did have some mates, it seems. One good friend, Willie t'Woodman, used to bring him the odd bit of something and they'd share a bite. But otherwise it was just Tom, living alone among the rocks and trees, and who knows why? I suppose it was what he chose to do, one day long in the past, and maybe he couldn't remember why any more, either. I suppose he might have been what we call a petty thief today, and a poacher.

The good thing about his home was that there was often plenty to eat - nuts and berries flourished in the valley, and the water, fresh from the hillsides, washed them down well. He could catch birds and rabbits, too. But Tom had known a family life once upon a time, and he was still partial to a wider diet than that. That's how he became known as an outlaw, because sometimes at night when he was feeling particularly peckish he would emerge from the forest, sneak on to a farm and then be off again, perhaps with a chicken or goose or two, like any old fox, or perhaps, less often, with a lamb or sheep, like any old thief. He was quick, but from what some people have said he was not quiet like a thief should be, for he dressed himself in rags with iron chains and shining brass ornaments pinned on them, and what a jingling, clinking, clanking racket they made! So people knew whenever Tom Bell was visiting their farm because of the noise, but however much they chased after him, they could never catch him. As if the night and the tangled trees and rocks weren't enough to deter pursuers, Tom Bell wore his boots back to front, so that he was never going where people thought he was going, though he'd always just been there. And of course, his cave had two entrances, one near Hebden Water and the other in the Colden valley, so he could always get out of one if someone found the other.

So nobody could catch him, and it was hard to find where he lived unless you'd been shown, and that was how Tom Bell liked it. For a long time he kept up this strange lonely lifestyle, cooking his spoils on a charcoal fire in his cave at night and sleeping off his meals by day.

One day two little children were off in the woods for an adventure, picking their way through the bushes and stones. Suddenly there was a noise, and they saw Willie t'Woodman walking through the trees, with a lamb in his arms. They decided to follow him, and Willie led them deeper into the wood.

Suddenly, Willie recoiled as two big black crows flew out of the bushes, one crying in loud uncouth tones, the other carrying something, something red and soft, in its beak. Just as scared as Willie, the children ducked behind a tree, and when they peeked out again they were just in time to see Willie run madly out from the bushes, and away as fast as his legs could carry him.

Well, the children wondered what had happened that had made Willie run away like that and in their curiosity they approached the bushes and found a crack in the rocks behind. A cave! They looked in, and they dared each other to go in, but neither would, until they agreed to go in together, hand-in-hand. They took a step or two inside, and they saw a light, a strange bluey-green light. In the light there was something else which they couldn't make out. And when the children thought they would look closer still, they noticed the smell. Oh, that cave smelt awful! There was the smell of smoke and of cooking and of something else that they didn't know, and hoped they'd never smell again. But their curiosity was still unsatisfied, and they ventured further forward, clutching their shirts over their noses.

The strange light seemed to come from a decaying tree root, and there was just enough of it to see a little in the cave. What they saw they would never forget for the rest of their lives. There was rubbish all around the cave - lots of bones, mostly, it seemed. There was a hearth, filled with black ashes, and beside the hearth there were more bones, and the remains of a cooked sheep. And there, beside the sheep, there was a pair of boots, and above the pair of boots was a shape dimly outlined in the strange light. They peered closer - and then they screamed when they realised what they were looking at, for the shape was that of a man, a very fat man, indeed, but a man who had, it seemed, been turned inside out! His stomach lay wide open! Suddenly they knew what the crows had been carrying! They knew what had made those noises they'd heard as they entered the cave! Still screaming, the children rushed out of the cave and back to their home. "Come quick" they told their parents, "we have seen something terrible".

So the parents went to the cave, and saw the same strange light that the children had seen, and they heard the same noises that the children had heard, and they smelt that same smell that the children had smelt, and then - they saw the same fearsome rotting body that the children had seen. They looked at the boots, and they saw that there was something funny about them - they had been put on back to front. And then they knew that it was the old outlaw, Tom Bell, lying there by his fire and the remains of his last meal. They fetched the constable, who hauled the body out of the cave, where the doctor, who was a bit of a religious man, could have a good look at it. News travelled fast, and a crowd had assembled, horrified and fascinated by the grisly corpse, by the time the doctor arrived.

"This man", he announced, "had eaten well before his death. In fact", he said, looking round at the assembled crowd, "he ate so well that it is my professional opinion that Tom Bell, for without doubt this is indeed that rogue, has actually burst *from overeating! This common thief did well out of us, stealing our livestock from our properties, and frightening us with his clanking and banging - but mark you all, the wages of sin, as you see before you, are* death! *Need you more proof?"*

The cave now known as Tom Bell's Cave may not be the 'original' one, but a name bestowed relatively recently by cavers. This cave is a passage between huge tumbled boulders, and takes a narrow zig-zag route into the earth for about ninety feet. Then there is a steep drop into a chamber for which climbing equipment is needed if you want to get out again - the only other possible exit is blocked by a boulder choke.

It is said that a carved stone head on the nearby Hebden Hey Scout Hut looks towards the entrance of the cave; the stone head has a piercing gaze that one might imagine would bore a cave in the hillside even if one weren't already there. When the old Scout Hut, a converted farmhouse, was taken down in the late 1970s, the orientation of its replacement preserved the direction of the head's gaze... but if we follow that stony gaze then or now, it certainly does not look towards today's Tom Bell's cave!

This story appears in a booklet first published in 1921[1], although I have heard the outline of the story - the outlaw, his cave, his reversed boots and his death by over-eating - from several informants. It was evidently frequently told in scout gatherings at Hebden Hey hostel[2].

The curious reference to Tom Bell's clanking appendages, which would make him anything but a sneak-thief, is probably an import to spice the tale up, but may have origins in either of two supernatural beings either side of the Pennines. Lancashire had a kind of boggart known as 'clap-cans', who goes around sounding like empty cans being beaten, while Yorkshire has 'Jack-in-Irons', a "being of great stature, wearing clanking chains" who liked (or likes?) to jump out on people in the dark[3].

An examination of the tale and any archaeological context traces a possible origin of the story to an incident in 1779, when a Rochdale thief, Joseph Bailey, was found hiding with the spoils of his work in a cave at Hathershelf Scout, at Mytholmroyd[4]. In line with known folkloric tendencies, the historical incident may then have been transferred, with almost literally bells on, to the cave in Hardcastle Crags, which may well have had pre-existing folklore attached to it.

In 1899, Herbert Cooper found a human skull in a crevice about twenty feet into the cave; he got out of the cave pretty quick and apparently it was another three weeks before he could be persuaded

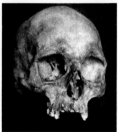

*The skull
(Courtesy of Hebden
Bridge Local History
Society)*

*Tom Bell's Cave
(Stan McCarthy)*

to crawl into the cave again to pull it out! Other contemporary cavers - one, J Helliwell, had left his or her name in a passage in the cave in 1817 - had spoken of the cave being "somewhat eerie and begetful of ghostly thoughts". The reports excited a great deal of local curiosity. Tourists went to inspect the cave, in the hopes of discovering some of Tom Bell's legendary booty, and there were tales of a rhino's skull and mummified cat also being found there; Cooper's brother, a sceptic, was the source for the cat report. The skull was shown to Dr Russell of Todmorden, and then to Prof. William Boyd Dawkins of Manchester University, who believed it to be probably prehistoric. It has now disappeared.

There are considerable doubts as to the authenticity of this find, of course, and a local businessman, Russell Dean, has certainly claimed that his grandfather put the skull in the cave. Even if it was a hoax, it was, like the stone head on Hebden Hey, in a known local tradition attaching special importance to skulls and carved heads[5]. Many prehistoric interments and rituals, including cave burials from the Stone and Bronze Ages, involved detaching the head from the other bones for separate treatment.

Given the description of the cave's location in some of the sources listed below, as well as the direction of the stone head's gaze, I have my doubts, as expressed above, whether everybody is talking about the same Tom Bell's Cave! I have not yet been able to find another candidate, however.

You could walk, according to local belief, through Tom Bell's cave into a tunnel that led through the hillside to Hell Hole Rocks or Choppy Knife Silk Mill; along the way, if you went through at the right time, you could hear people stoking their fires in Heptonstall. It's also said that in the nineteenth century, after the loss of a child in the tunnel - or possibly only the fear of such loss - the entrance was walled up. In the Colden Valley, below Heptonstall, there is a cave at Hell Hole Rocks which goes some way towards the basements of Heptonstall - but that, like our Tom Bell's Cave, is choked by a rock fall - always a danger in this kind of cave[6].

This story has developed many versions and contains many twists and turns concerning the discovery of the skull - Cooper the caver, for instance, owned a teashop in the Crags, and was set to benefit from the increased tourism! Or are we too cynical nowadats? See the listed sources, and make up your own mind!

1. D T Wilcock, 'Stories & Folklore from the District called Hardcastle Crags'
2. For versions of the tale, see also Kendall, Porritt, and newspaper references below. Broadbent made a romanticised poem of the tale, with some of its more lurid episodes, which also appeared in the *Hebden Bridge Times* and in part in Kendall. More recently, Paul Weatherhead has made a new thorough investigation of the whole episode.
3. Wright: 194
4. Heginbottom & Gilks, 1989
5. See Billingsley, 1998
6. For caving information, please see Brook *et al*

Billingsley, John. *A Stony Gaze: investigating Celtic and other stone heads*. Capall Bann, 1998
Broadbent, W. *A selection from the miscellaneous poems*, Todmorden 1841, 53-5
Brook, D, Davies, G M, & Ryder, P F. *Northern Caves Vol. 5*, p.141

Heginbottom, J A & Gilks, J A. 'A Note on the History and Archaeology of Tom Bell's Cave, Hardcastle Crags', in *Halifax Antiquarian Society Transactions* 1989, pp.1-6.
Hebden Bridge Times and Calder Vale Gazette, May 12, October 20, November 10 & November 24, 1899; and February 2, 1900
Kendall, H P. 'Tom Bell's cave, a Heptonstall Legend', in *Halifax Antiquarian Society Transactions* 1902
Porritt, Arthur. *It Happened Here 2nd Series*. Wade 1975, pp.170-71
Tickner, Max. 'Down and Down - to the cave of Old Tom Bell', *Halifax Weekly Courier and Guardian*, February 10, 1967
Weatherhead, Paul. *Weird Calderdale*. Tom Bell Pub., 2004
Wilcock, D T. *Stories from Hardcastle Crags & Heptonstall No. 1*. 1919
Wilcock, D T. *Stories & Folklore from the District called Hardcastle Crags*. 1921
Wright, Elizabeth Mary. *Rustic Speech and Folklore*, Milford/Oxford University Press 1913, p.194

8.
THE MILLER'S GRAVE

Around three thousand years ago, give or take a few centuries, local Bronze Age settlers built a number of sites on Midgley Moor. Some were, no doubt, designed to bury their dead - although in the acid soil of the moor, next to nothing much will remain of bodies after all this time. One of the largest and most visible of these Bronze Age remains is today known as the Miller's Grave, and it is just one of several sites that seem to indicate that the moor was something of a 'ritual landscape' in prehistory.

Nearer the present, the mound became the site for another ritual burial, one that gave it its present name, the Miller's Grave.

> He wasn't the first, and he won't be the last, but that doesn't lessen the tragedy of Miller Lee, who plunged into the depths of despair when he was spurned by a sweetheart late in the eighteenth century. When he was found hanged at Mayroyd Mill in Hebden Bridge, it seemed clear that he was one of those who could not bear to live with the grief.
>
> Yet if it was peace he wanted, it was not easily to be obtained. The church at that time deemed that those who had taken their own life were undeserving of Christian burial and so he was denied a place in the parish churchyard at Heptonstall. Instead, his body was taken up the Midgley hillside to Four Lane Ends, on the Heights Road between Mount Skip and Foster Clough, at the edge of Midgley Moor. Here, where a track leading from Mytholmroyd to the moors crosses Heights Road, a trench was dug and the shrouded body of Miller Lee was laid down, unmarked and unblessed at the crossroads.
>
> Heights Road was a lot busier in those days, and Four Lane Ends was a spot frequently passed by locals both day and night. What they thought about Lee's burial there is unknown, but as time passed they had more and more reason to make remark on it. People reported a presence there that frightened them - they said it was a haunted spot, that Miller Lee was

'walking'. Apprehension and downright loathing of the spot grew, and angry resentful words were spoken about the miller and his dreadful persistence in this world. "He should be moved", people cried, but the church authorities were adamant - one who takes their own life has no place in consecrated ground.

This, of course, did not satisfy the villagers, and finally a mob gathered at the dead of night by torchlight beside the grave to do something about their complaint. Several had brought spades and tools, and they set to exhuming the miller's body. There were some present who tried to stop this desecration, but they were driven away with sticks and stones, and were unable to prevent the rotting body of Lee returning to the night air, where he was welcomed with kicks and other rough treatment. Resentment had run high and respected the dead no more, in their eyes, than the dead had respected the villagers. The body was wrapped and hoisted up and away on to the moor. The villagers were taking him somewhere, they thought, where he could be of no more nuisance.

Nearly half a mile away across the rough heather terrain, they laid him down again, and committed him back to earth in the old mound we now know as Miller's Grave. This was an old burial mound of a people long gone, along with their pagan beliefs, and far enough from the road that Lee's spectre could surely bother none other than a few sheep. The crowd went home, confident of a good night's work that had dealt with their problem.

Can we be surprised, however, after such treatment, that Miller Lee still did not rest easy? The haunting did not stop, and the locals could sleep no more soundly, nor walk less in dread of the moor edge. "We've done our best", they cried, "and he still won't leave us be. Lee should not be our problem - he should be moved".

The outcry was such that the church authorities conferred, and relented. Lee had made a special case, they decided, and space would be made for him in Heptonstall churchyard. So in an unmarked grave in an unknown corner of the churchyard, Miller Lee finally came to rest in peace. And on the opposite hillside, the inhabitants of Midgley once more slept soundly.

The remains of the Bronze Age round barrow, Miller's Grave, with Robin Hood's Pennystone in the background

Suicide is one of the traditional religious taboos, and anyone who took their own life was considered to have placed themselves beyond the pale of normal social and religious conventions. A mark of this disfavour was that they were not to be buried in churchyards, nor to have a Christian service read over their funeral. Their proper place was considered to be in unconsecrated ground, land foreign to God, where gather ghosts, witches, fairies and other beings that frequent in the shadowy space between this world and another. Such threshold zones are called 'liminal', meaning 'at the edge'; and all thresholds have this magical ability to become gateways for passage between worlds. This notion has been current since prehistory and can be traced archaeologically in the locations of rituals such as foundation sacrifice and votive deposits, and folklorically in a wealth of traditions and beliefs. Prime amongst such places, however, is the crossroads, where traditionally more than our three dimensions, more than our humankind, meet. The blues singer, Robert Johnson, famously and apocryphally learned to play the guitar by going to a crossroads at midnight - a liminal time at a liminal place.

This story reaffirms this esoteric status of crossroads and their role in the burial of suicide victims; it was common practice until 1823 that they be interred in the highway, and crossroads were generally chosen. This is locally recorded in Halifax; workmen digging in Parkinson Lane in 1859 found the skeleton of Elizabeth Gill, who had poisoned herself. They also found the piece of wood that had staked her down in her grave, a practice to prevent the unquiet ghost 'walking', and a public rite of disgrace. Also near the lower crossroads in Parkinson Lane is Goldsmith's Grave (recorded 1652), where Richard Commons, an Irish goldsmith who hanged himself, was interred[1].

The law did, however, allow for suicide victims to be buried in consecrated ground if they were adjudged to be mentally unbalanced at the time; in such cases the Church was given the power of decision, and if admitted to a churchyard, the body would be placed on its north side; perhaps this is a clue to why Heptonstall church finally accepted Lee. His tale also indicates, though, that the mound, a pagan ritual site, was seen as a liminal location, a threshold between worlds, and thus outside the realm of Christianity.

Although few prehistoric sites are marked on Ordnance Survey maps, Midgley Moor, and indeed all of upper Calderdale, is rich in archaeological remains of the Bronze Age[2]. The concentration of sites on this moorland plateau implies that this was a ritual zone for those distant forebears, a perception that has passed down the centuries. It may also be noted in passing that a bearing from Robin Hood's Pennystone - the large boulder visible from Miller's Grave - towards the mound shows 135°, suggestive of a winter solstice sunrise orientation.

The bare bones of this story - if you'll pardon the pun - were found in a book rather than word of mouth; in this case, Watson's *History of Halifax*. I am indebted to Mike Haslam for pointing out a more plausible location for Four Lane Ends in old Midgley township, which makes more sense than my previous assumed location in Midgley village. Suicide burials were, understandably, usually on the edges of existing settlements, rather than within them; and from Four Lane Ends the old mound is considerably nearer - handy if you're carrying a decomposing body.

Robert Law, however, in 1897 noted that "The tradition relating to the origin of this name [Miller's Grave] varies somewhat amongst the people of the countryside" and gave another variant. In this version, John the Miller from Luddenden was taking a short cut home across the moor. It was, as seems almost required of a moorland story, a dark and stormy night. He had been at market, and his pockets were well laden with cash; and near Crow Hill he was ambushed, robbed and murdered by a gang who then buried his body in the tumulus.

Law's comment about local variants of the tale explaining the name of the Miller's Grave underscores my point in the introduction, that any legend may have other versions, and who is to say which is the correct one? If, indeed, any are correct, and if, indeed, it matters. Michael Haslam, again, has said the correct version of a tale is the one you have heard yourself, and on one level perhaps that must be true.

1. Clarke, 1993; Hanson, 1923; Porritt, 1975, pp.126-7
2. For more archaeological information on Midgley Moor and the local Bronze Age, see Barnes; Billingsley & Bennett, 1996; Faull & Moorhouse; Shepherd.

Barnes, Bernard. *Man and the Changing Landscape*. Merseyside County Council/University of Liverpool, 1982

Billingsley, John & Bennett, Paul. 'Recent Fieldwork on Midgley Moor'. *Northern Earth* 65, 1996

Clarke, Neil. pers. comm. & *Calderdale Earth Mysteries Group Newsletter* 1993

Faull, L L & Moorhouse, S A. *West Yorkshire; an Archaeological Survey to AD 1500, Vol. 1*. West Yorkshire Metropolitan County Council, 1981

Hanson, T W, 'Some Halifax Houses: Parkinson House', *Halifax Antiquarian Society Transactions* 1923

Haslam, Mike. Pers. comm. & 'A Boundary Stone on Midgley Moor'. *Calder Valley Press* 4, June 1979

Law, Robert. 'Evidences of Prehistoric man on the Moorlands in and around the Parish of Halifax', *Halifax Naturalist* Vol.2/7, April 1897, p.1-2

Porritt, Arthur. *It Happened Here* 2nd Series. Fred Wade, 1975

Shepherd, David. 'Prehistoric Activity in the Central South Pennines'. *Halifax Antiquarian Society Transactions* 2004, pp.13-38

Shepherd, David. 'Local Monuments, for Local People'. *Northern Earth* 98, 2004

Shepherd, David. 'Stand by your Stone'. *Northern Earth* 107, 2006

Simpson, Jacqueline, & Roud, Steve. *A Dictionary of English Folklore*. Oxford University Press, 2000

9.
CHURN MILK JOAN

A lonely stone,
afloat in the stone heavings of emptiness,
keeps telling her tale

This is how Ted Hughes begins his poem, 'Churn Milk Joan', in his powerful Calderdale cycle, *Remains of Elmet*.
Hughes, born in the village of Mytholmroyd at the foot of the hillside below Midgley Moor, was drawn to the moors even as a child, and the standing stone on the fringe of the moor is as much a landmark for us as it was for Hughes in the 1930s.
This is no prehistoric menhir, but it stands nearly seven feet tall and acts like a folklore conductor, attracting tales towards it. Let us call this stone, like the Bridestone, 'she', as her name, after all, is Churn Milk Joan.

Churn Milk Joan, with Crow Hill behind

There was an old inn called the Mount Skip at the edge of Midgley Moor that was frequently visited by travellers as well as the hard-drinking quarrymen that worked on Cock Hill right above. The Heights Road was a lot busier then than it is today, as indeed was the inn, until somebody decided they could make more money, and quicker, by turning it into cottages than by selling beer to the locals, but that's another story, and rather newer than ours.

Traditional inns, of course, sold whatever fare travellers needed - ale, spirits, beverages and victuals of all kinds - and in the days before preservatives, fridges and freezers they needed constant stocking up with provisions to keep their customers satisfied. That didn't mean a shopping trip, usually, and certainly there was no question of jumping into your 4WD for a trip to the superstore; what you had to do was ride or walk to the nearest farm that had what was required.

So when the milk for the day was needed, the maid at Mount Skip, a girl called Joan, was sent out to collect it. She could have gone along Heights Road, then just a stony track, but she was a local lass and knew the moors, and the quickest route was along the edge of the moor. So this morning off she went as usual to the farm and picked up the churn of milk set aside for the Skip. Well, it wasn't very far back to the inn, and she'd done the milk run in bad weather many's the time, so when she dallied a little at the farm and was running slightly late, she paid no heed to the gathering clouds - she knew the moor well enough.

But the blizzard that caught her cared naught for paths, and the snow that fell was thicker than fog. It blew right into her face as she struggled through the heather and Joan began to lose her bearings. She was lost, it seemed, and she was bitterly cold. Even her petticoats were beginning to freeze up, with a hem of heavy ice all round her boots. Joan began to worry, fighting off panic as the blizzard continued. Suddenly and at last she was relieved to see a shape in front of her, and recognised it as the old boundary stoop near Nelmires - it had taken her longer to get here than it should have done, but as she passed it she felt a bit more secure, though her heart still beat furiously and she was anxious to get back to the inn. She stepped firmly out again, but the land drops quickly just there, and in the drifting snow it was hard to tell. Over Joan went, unbalanced by her load - too heavily she fell, feet first, taking the wind out of her, and she watched as the heavy churn fell too, and toppled over her...

And the milk spilled unnoticed over the snow and around her body.

Now, the people at the inn were naturally concerned, but while the storm raged there was nothing to be done but hope that the girl had decided to wait it out at the farm. When the weather cleared up and she still didn't return, however, they went out to search the moor, as folk had too often done before.

Joan's body, pale and frozen stiff into the snowdrifts, lay near the stone, beside her a near-empty churn of milk and a faint stain in the snow. And that, they say, is how that old Nelmires Stoop got a new name.

I heard this story numerous times after I moved to Mytholmroyd, about the milk-maid who died and lost her milk at this spot - the only variation was that some said she had been overcome by a storm, others by fog, others by snow. I have therefore incorporated all three into this story, but have preferred snow as the dominant weather - the visually poetic aesthetic of fresh milk spilling on to new-fallen snow has a poignant appeal.

Churn Milk Joan may also have been a provider of pocket money to some local children, at least when they got to a certain height. For if you stand on the stone at her foot, and reach your hands up towards her crown, you will find a basin in the top of the pillar; and if you are lucky you will find some coins there. What you are supposed to do is to remove those coins and replace them with coins of equal or greater value from your own pocket, in order to ensure good fortune in the coming months. This practice has been around for some while, at least since the 1930s, when Crump recalled it[1]. This is an exciting kind of custom - what will I find there? (and I once dipped my hand into a pile of frog spawn someone had put in the basin!) - and it will clearly appeal to children as much as, if not more than, adults (as long as they can reach the top of the stone); and moreover it clearly shows the function of folklore not just to entertain, but also to teach. For the moral of the exchange custom is never to take without giving equal or better measure, and therein lies the secret of good fortune - the trust of your

A ritual performance: checking the financial state of Joan's crown

neighbours and those you do business with. Nonetheless I have come across youngsters, even with their parents, slipping the 5p or so into their own pockets, with their elders' full connivance. Think on, parents!

A nearby farmer, now dead, told a lady I met at the stone one day that the custom of putting money on the stone started because there was not enough money to pay for Joan's funeral; according to another acquaintance, the farmer told him that he took the money himself to pay for fresh flowers for the girl's grave in Luddenden churchyard, which is how come bouquets appeared on the grave of a girl who died long ago and had no known family in the area. I have been unable to ascertain whether such a grave really existed, but I was told that Jimmy had hoped his sons would carry on the custom - whether they do so or not I do not know. Another informant told me that in the 1970s there was a man who collected the money on the stone to have a drink in the tea shop that was on the way to Cragg Vale's Robin Hood Inn - or was it in the pub itself?

Wherever the money went, this would appear at first meeting to be in origin a penny-stone or plague stone custom, deriving from the days when plague was rife. Then, traders would meet inhabitants of infected townships at a well-known spot somewhere outside the settlement, and do their business there. All money changing hands was passed through a basin of vinegar as disinfectant, and often water-worn basins on top of stones would provide a suitable receptacle.

Further on over Midgley Moor, Robin Hood's Pennystone has a suitable basin which is far more accessible than Joan's. Although sometimes you can find a coin there, it is not the Pennystone that holds the custom today, but Churn Milk Joan. Has the tradition at some point migrated from Robin's somewhat remote stone to Joan's, nearer the road? Churn Milk Joan is, after all, really too tall for a pennystone in the plague stone sense - neither trader nor customer could see what it is in the basin, a point made all too unpleasantly by my frog spawn experience! Or is there something else going on?

The question is whether we are correct in ascribing our local pennystones (there used to be another Robin Hood's Pennystone at Wainstalls, which we will discuss in the next volume of Calderdale folk tales) to trading venues during epidemics. The citizens of Halifax in 1539 complained of certain ne'er-do-wells playing "at the pennistone... an unlawful game" that "pulls down men's walls"[2], and this gives a clue to an alternative explanation. Pennystone was a kind of quoits, and involved throwing stones at a penny balanced on a peg - hence, 'pennystone'. The preferred stone was approximately round and flat, a bit like a discus, or indeed a quoit; in the quest for a suitable stone, one might well imagine that stone walls were at risk. As some of Calderdale's Robin Hood legends make reference to the hero playing quoits with stones (again a topic to be returned to in the next volume), it seems most likely that the local pennystones refer not to plague stones, but to substitute quoits for this old and unlawful pastime; and while smaller wall stones would have sufficed for ordinary folk, isolated large boulders might be attributed to the games of one of the old and literally larger-than-life culture heroes - like Robin Hood[3].

While this might account neatly for the pennystones, however, it does not explain why a custom so clearly related to the plague stone usage should have sprung up at Churn Milk Joan. We may need to look for the answer in a more contrived scenario; perhaps someone familiar with plague stones and their alternative name of pennystones imported the cash exchange custom at some point to this standing stone, with an aim in mind. The little ritual comprised not only a kind of game and incentive for children to take the air on the moors[4], but also had the educational value mentioned above.

*Robin Hood's Pennystone,
Wainstalls, in 1761
(From John Watson's 1789
History of Halifax)*

And now, whatever the origin of these names and customs, they have passed into local tradition at this inspirational stone, along with still others.

A much bleaker version of the Churn Milk Joan story is related by the Poet Laureate, Ted Hughes. He grew up in Mytholmroyd in the 1930s, and in the poem he tells of the pennystone custom, and then of Joan's sad fate - but the story he knew was that 'foxes killed her'. His poem also suggests a play on 'Joan' - that it may be 'jamb', and the stone thus seen as a doorway through which fate can operate, a liminal threshold over which Joan - and perhaps the foxes - passed. Interestingly, this connection of Joan-jamb was also made by the poet Michael Haslam, who lives nearby on the edge of the moor.

Recently, I heard yet another variant of the story, from a man born and bred in Mytholmroyd. He told me that the story that he and his friends knew alleged that Joan was what some call, euphemistically, a 'hospitality girl', known for giving certain favours to men (perhaps she and Nan Moor of the Bridestones tale had something in common?). Her own trade was in butter-making, hence Churn Milk Joan, but because of her free sexuality she was called a witch, and no doubt other things besides - for my informant's tale ended that she was done away with by one of her lovers here on the moor, "maybe six hundred years ago", and the stone recalls her fate. This version, however, seems to be unfamiliar to most of the local people I have asked.

Watson does not mention any version of this story in his encyclopaedic *History and Antiquities of the Parish of Halifax* (1775), so if any of the tales were current in his time, they - unusually, it must be said - failed to reach his ears.

When we hear stories like this, it is natural to ask questions like 'Is any of it true? Did Joan die there? If so, how?'. And we would be most likely to feel that it is just a story made up about a fictitious individual to explain the curious name of this stone. However, a few years ago I went to visit a friend in the South of France, a woman with a considerable ability in psychism, and interest in old stones. I took along some photographs of suitable places in the valley, to give her an idea of the area I live in. When she came to the photo of Churn Milk Joan, she immediately held the photo away from her and exclaimed "John! Why have you given me this? Someone's been killed here!". Make what you will of this; but when I heard the story of the farmer putting flowers on the grave, I wondered if perhaps there really had been a 'Joan'.

Recently, a friend has told me that when she took a group of ladies walking on Midgley Moor, several of them recoiled when she touched the stone, and warned her that it was not a good thing to do!

Churn Milk Joan bears a bench-mark arrow on its east face and some enigmatic cup marks; on the west face is a very worn date, perhaps 1785, and only visible at all in certain light conditions. A similar 18th-century date is clearly visible on the Greenwood Stone, further across the moor. These inscribed dates may be related to Wadsworth boundary perambulations carried out by staff and pupils of Heptonstall Grammar School in 1778 and other years[5].

It is a boundary stone with a history dating back to around 1590 and a boundary dispute between Sir George Savile, Lord of Wadsworth, and John Lacy, Lord of Midgley. On a map drawn up by Christopher Saxton in 1602 to record the settlement of the dispute, a 'merestone' (boundary stone) is marked at Foster Clough Head, and this is the stone that became Churn Milk Joan.

The first appearance of the present name on a map seems to be Myers' map of 1834-5. In the 18th century it would appear to have been known as Nelmires Stoop, Nelmires being the ruin visible a couple of fields away to the SW. A 1956 OS map shows the stone as also called 'Savile's Low', but Haigh demonstrates that this is an error, and that Savile's Low is a separate boundary point some distance away, which in origin may be the oldest point on the boundary, perhaps a prehistoric cairn[6]. An earlier Saxton map, drawn up in 1594, does not show the stone. It seems safe to assume that the erection of Churn Milk Joan therefore took place at some point between 1594 and 1602.

If you squat down at Churn Milk Joan and look to the north, you will see a small notch in the horizon and the faint trace of a straight ditch leading to it from the stone, which you can still follow. This was first shown and explained to me as a ley line, but is evidently the remains of the boundary ditch! It does however lead towards the other named sites on Midgley Moor - Robin Hood's Pennystone, Miller's Grave and the Greenwood Stone (also on Saxton's 1602 boundary map). At the far end of the boundary, on the old track known as Limer's Gate, is another similar standing stone, known as Wadsworth Law, at High Brown Knoll, and hikers occasionally leave coins on top of this stone too.

Churn Milk Joan is said to turn round three times at New Year, on hearing the sound of the church bell at Mytholmroyd or Sowerby, depending on whose version you hear; this is a common tale type associated with standing stones, and is part of a wider repertoire of tales about stones acquiring the power to move at certain points of the year. By contrast, she was a fixed pillar around which Mytholmroyd children held hands and circled, while making a wish, at least until the 1950s, though how far back this goes is unknown.

'Churn Milk', according to Halliwell Sutcliffe, is a Yorkshire Dales term for the kernel of a nut before it ripens. Elizabeth Mary Wright speaks of a wood-spirit, Churn Milk Peg, whose job it is to protect unripe nuts from being gathered too soon by children; apparently she is also "wont to beguile her leisure by smoking a pipe"[7]! However, there is a local usage of 'churn milk', meaning buttermilk, which is a far more likely origin of the name.

1. Crump, p.76
2. *Halifax Guardian Historical Almanack*, 1913, pp. 82-83
3. With thanks to Jeremy Harte for his help in teasing out this thread.
4. Mothers of Midgley used to take children with coughs and colds to the nearby Folly Field, below Crow Hill - believed to be a sure cure, as recalled in verse by Audrey Buckley (born in Midgley, 1924):
   Up there, there were a cure
   the wind were strong and bracing
   and very very pure
   y'see, that wind did cure you
   whatever you did ail
   I don't know why it did
   but it never seemed to fail
   (oral history recording loaned courtesy of Peggy Horsfield)
5. Haigh, 1991.
6. Haigh, 1991
7. Contrary to information given in a recent book on old Yorkshire stones, deriving from a misreading of one of the sources below, our Churn Milk Joan has *never* been known as Churn Milk Peg.

Billingsley, John. 'Churn Milk Joan'. *Northern Earth* 65, 1996.

Billingsley, John. 'Families, Friends & Neighbours: Folklore & cultural tradition in Midgley', in I Bailey, D Cant & A Petford (eds), *Aspects of Midgley History*, 2007 forthcoming.

Crump, W B , *The Little Hill Farm*, Scrivener Press, London 1949, p.76.

Faull, L L & Moorhouse, S A. *West Yorkshire; an Archaeological Survey to AD 1500, Vol. 2*, p.276. West Yorkshire Metropolitan County Council, 1981.

Haigh, D. ' 'Fax Fallacies', *Halifax Antiquarian Society Transactions* 1991, pp.125-135.

Harwood, H W. 'Glimpses of Midgley History', unpub MS, n.d., in Halifax Archives MISC 78/54

Haslam, Mike. 'A Boundary Stone on Midgley Moor', *Calder Valley Press* 4, June 1979.

Hebden Bridge Times, Oct. 8, 1954.

Hughes, Ted. 'Churn Milk Joan', *Remains of Elmet*. Faber, 1979.

Sutcliffe, Halliwell. *The Striding Dales*. Frek Warne & Co, n.d.

Watson, Rev. John. *The History of the Town and Parish of Halifax*, Milner, Halifax, 1789.

Wright, Elizabeth Mary. *Rustic Speech and Folklore*. Milford/OUP, 1913, p.198.

Thanks to Ann Adamson, Emrys Ashley, Stephen Beasley, David Greenwood, Dave Hamer, Jeremy Harte, Mike Haslam, Steve Marsden, members of the Mytholmroyd Historical Society and several others whose names I never learned for details relating to this story, and the accompanying notes.

10.
PLACES AND TRACES

The stories collected and retold in this book and the next in the series are those legends which have survived with enough information to comprise something like a complete narrative. More often, however, place legends today are fragmentary references to events or beliefs associated with a certain location, and every locality, rural or urban, has a selection of such 'storied places'. This chapter brings together such fragments and also other pieces of local folklore relating to places in the upper valley.

Here Be Dragons
Place legends are more than simply tales of something that happened (or more correctly, are said to have happened) at a certain place. The occurrence they celebrate may be major or minor, they may be held to have occurred in some distant past, or even in recent memory; but as they pass further into community history - the well of memory in which they must find their own way to float, or sink - their link with actual events tends to become increasingly tenuous. As it retreats from fact, it more closely approaches the local perception of place. Typically, a place legend or similar place-related lore not only gives an account of an event in the local subcultural history, it also in some way characterises or is characterised by the place.

Sometimes the story or association has vanished, but leaves behind a placename, itself a powerful factor in identifying that place in the local psyche, and almost as good as a legend in characterising that place.

We can collect various sorts of fragments concerning 'what might have happened where'. The true place legend, however, takes things a step further, often into almost mythical territory; it becomes a landmark on what we might call a 'cognitive map' of the area, a mental map held broadly in common by those that live in that area. In such a map, the locality is the known world, outside it is a less certain, even perhaps scary out-world; at its margins we can expect to encounter inscriptions that recognise marginality, like

'Here Be Dragons'. "This is the world we know and can tell you about", it says, "but we can't tell you about the world beyond, neither about its hazards nor its stories". For the Calder Valley, the Pendle Witches or the Giant of Rombald's Moor are as good as dragons, and far enough away. It was enough for people to deal with a bunch of local boggarts, Tom Bell, and Robin Hood tossing stones about, and other local stories warned people about the potential hazards of the surrounding landscape. Beyond? - don't even go there!

Note, for instance, how often the weather plays a role in our upland stories - so much so that it arguably constitutes another character in the narratives, an unpredictable and ultimate bogeyman, alongside the human protagonists. Also, the frequency of placenames relating to the various varieties of little people are eloquent testimony to what people thought about the farther shores of the world around them.

Place legends are therefore an essential part of local history, but often they venture into undocumented and unquantifiable territory where many local historians fear to tread. Much of such material seems to derive from memorates, accounts of a magical or religious content, or from a belief in a parallel supernatural world with its own denizens living alongside us. Such perceptions seem to separate these places from the everyday world and locate them in a mental otherworld (whatever the reality may be of a real 'out-there' otherworld). It cannot be pointed out too often, of course, that our modern rationalist preferences fly in the face of millennia of received wisdom. Whether you or I accept the reality of such magical or supernatural realms is entirely irrelevant - the fact is that generations upon generations of our forebears believed that they were living cheek-by-jowl with another realm of existence, that created strange anomalies in everyday life, and they had the witness statements to prove it to their satisfaction.

Dragons are locally an example of this reduction into placenames. We have in Calderdale only one dragon tale (none at all in the upper valley), and that extremely fragmentary - in the 1920s a local writer was told that "a right long time ago" a wood at Blakelaw, near Hartshead, had been home to a dragon[1]. An even longer time ago, however, the element 'worm' (from *wyrm*, 'reptile') appeared in a few local placenames - Wormecliffe (later Onecliff) in Greetland was recorded in 1356, Wormeley in Ovenden was recorded in 1462, and Wormewall in Barkisland was recorded in 1402. 'Worm' is frequently encountered in dragonlore; the Lambton and Wharncliffe Crags dragons, for instance, were known as worms. Moreover, a field called Dragontayle was recorded in 1573^2, and the wood at Blakelaw may once have been known as Dracanhlawe. Are these placenames the only surviving remains of local legendary beasts, or at least the belief in them?

Other legends and folklore concerning places speak of the character of the community. Naturally, such stories may often put an incident in a more favourable light than, say, neighbouring communities would - for instance, one community's 'daring raid' in, perhaps, sneaking into a village after dark to steal their maypole (a common form of village rivalry in the past) will become, for the victim community, a 'cowardly act when people were asleep'. In a more local example, the story of the Devil being unable to gain a foothold on the Great Rock implies he was unable to gain a foothold in Blackshaw Head or Stansfield township - whereas he stood a better chance in *some* places. The point of issue with so much of folklore, again, is the perception of the event or story by the people concerned - and again uncomfortably for those who like their history cut and dried, the truth lies somewhere in between the lines.

But the truth does not always serve the necessary function of keeping a community together and self-aware. Thus, the stories and tales that grow up around a community constitute a phenomenological experience of enhanced meaning within the mundane lived environment - in other words, life is experienced as a lived-in thing in which certain times, places and memories feature more strongly than others, and separate out from the everyday environment. This is a dimension that is so much a part of everyday life that neither customary 'common sense' nor documentary sources can easily address it.

The fragments that follow, then, are not always stories as such, but pieces of a jigsaw that, if we could only construct it in its entirety, would constitute a 'cognitive map' of upper Calderdale - place/event interfaces that we come to know not through personal experience, but by hearsay and by being here.

1. H N & M Pobjoy, *The Story of the Ancient Parish of Hartshead-cum-Clifton*, Ridings Pub, 1972, p.7.
2. Smith, A H. *Placenames of the West Riding of Yorkshire: iii Morley wapentake*. CUP, 1961; N.B. Wormstall in Ovenden is ascribed to 'warm stall').

The Devil and some Spurious Saints

People say that the Devil was a regular visitor around here. In our dialect, you know, 'devil' sounds like 'duel', and that's why you'll find places like Dulesgate up by Tod, or Tuel Lane in Sowerby Bridge - because people met the devil there, you see.

Placenames can be one way of divining legendary sites, though sometimes the legends themselves may have vanished. When we hear of Tuel Lane, for instance, and know that 'Tuel' is a local dialect name for the Devil, we must surely wonder why it was given such an uninviting name. What story have we lost there, and at Dulesgate, too, another Devil's track, on the Todmorden-Bacup road, or at Dule Hole Bank in Rishworth? Is Old Harry Lane in Mytholmroyd *that* Old Harry? We may not know the stories that led to such names, but we may suspect that something about them was well enough known at one time for people to give them such associations. We have, of course, already looked at two places associated with the Devil - Great Rock and Stoodley Pike.

The Devil has always been a respected architect and engineer in folk tradition and numerous bridges are attributed to him. In such cases, these were probably not places where one might run into the old fiend, but where he is given the credit for impressive engineering beyond normal human undertakings. To have handiwork ascribed to the Devil rather than the actual artisans may seem unfair to those long-ago workers, but it is no mean accolade! Locally, his major work of this sort is the Dhoul's Pavement, or the Devil's Pavement, the paved stone causeway across Blackstone Edge.

De'il Scout, in the Colden Valley, is a rock outcrop that offers a simulacrum, or likeness, of a giant face looking out from the hillside. Points of land that give good vantage points are often called 'Scout', like Scout Rock above Mytholmroyd. Here, then, it could have been seen as a good watchtower for the (or a) Devil - or the rocky face itself may have been seen as the Devil.

I suppose these hills suited some men who looked for God in the wilderness, and there were hermits here, I've heard. Like St Toby, or Tobias some say, who lived in a cave up at Eaves. And they even say Thomas a Becket passed through one time, and left a well for the people in Wadsworth - Pecket Well, as now is.

Where you find the Devil, there you may find saints, but which are the more numerous? In Calderdale, it would probably be devils, as we have few saints, and those we have seem questionable. Pecket Well is obviously named after a local well or spring, though which one is not now certain; it seems likely to have been the now-lost spring between the village and the war memorial. Nonetheless, local tales have attributed 'Pecket' to 'Becket', and have claimed variously that 'Becket Well' was one from which the martyr St Thomas a Becket drank when passing through the area, or that it was one that he miraculously caused to appear. The notion of a saintly foundation is a common legend associated with holy wells. Passing saints, especially in 'Celtic' areas like Wales and Brittany, have struck staves into the ground, lost their head or been involved in other acts which have caused springs to gush miraculously forth[3]. The Becket tale here is almost certainly a deliberate importation of this tale type, assisted by the dedication of the old Heptonstall church to the martyr. There is no record that Becket ever visited this part of Yorkshire, nor that the village well was any kind of holy well, but it was a popular idea, and in the 19th century writers and newspapers commonly made reference to Becket or Becket's Well; an 1894 guide refers to "the village of Becket's Well, vulgarly called Pecket Well" and states it is certain that it "is a very ancient hamlet, as the well is dedicated to the patron saint of the parish, St Thomas a Becket"[4].

While on wells and suspicious saints, it is worth noting the house now called St Ambrose Well, off Wadsworth Lane below the old Mount Skip Inn above Hebden Bridge. Until the 1980s, this house was known as Ambry Well, from which its present name of St Ambrose Well was fancifully derived; 'ambry' is actually local dialect for 'closet' or 'cupboard', and aptly enough the two water outlets in the garden of the house are situated in closet-sized well-houses! The 1854 Ordnance Survey map identifies the lower outlet as Ambry Well[5] and St Ambrose is the result of some artful renaming!

Another elusive saint - one whose deeds, according to a well-known aphorism, may be better known to God than to Man (but even then I rather doubt it) - is St Tobias, who was said to have lived in a cave among the evocative crags that line the top of the Colden Valley at Eaves Edge below Heptonstall. He wouldn't be the valley's only hermit, if such he was, but the Halifax hermit whose lust led him to cut off a young girl's head (a tale to be told in our second volume of local place legends) has not given them - or at least the legendary ones - the best of reputations locally.

There have been hermits in the valley, of course, whose lifestyle may not have entirely fitted them to the saintly stereotype preferred in these more modern and demanding days (and we will hear of these, too, in Volume Two), but who seem to have been suitably pious and unassuming, if not exactly pure, in their lifestyle - men like John Preston, 'of no fixed abode', but a familiar figure in Luddenden Dean in the mid-19th century, where he would frequently preach at Luddenden Dean Spa on the first Sunday in May. John surely became almost legendary, at least, in his sayings and way of life; and one wonders how distant the ancient holy hermits actually were from his adopted tramp-like existence[6].

3. Janet Bord, *Cures & Curses: Ritual & Cult at Holy Wells*, Heart of Albion, 2006, pp.113-121.
4. *Guide to Hardcastle Crags, Hebden Bridge & Neighbourhood*, Moss Printeries, 1894, p.7. See also Rev H Wild, *Holiday Walks in the N Countree*, nd, p146; Hebden *Bridge Times*, 11 Oct 1882; John Stansfeld, *History of the Family of Stansfeld of Stansfield*. Goodall & Suddick, Leeds, 1885.
5. See J A Heginbottom, 'Early Christian Sites in Calderdale', *HAS* 1988, p.9.
6. See Whiteley Turner, *A Springtime Saunter*, 1913, repub. M T D Rigg, Pub, Leeds 1986, p.5-12.

Boggarts and their like

There's no telling what a boggart may get up to, just the first thing that pops into its head, it seems. Some of them were alright, but some were a plain nuisance. Today we might call them fancy names like poltergeist, but back then, if something boggarty happened, well then, it was a boggart at the root of it.

An astonishing variety of otherworldly beings are traditionally thought to have shared our living spaces, indoors and out. Their apparent lack of material substance prevents any general agreement on appearance or identification, but there is no shortage of rumours concerning the deeds of what are often known as the 'little people' - even though many of them are far from little - or 'fairy folk'. The most common name in northern England for the culprit behind inexplicable and unsettling experiences is the boggart, and as I noted in 'The Cliviger Boggart' we have no shortage of them in this area. The boggart is a kind of brownie, but there were others of its kin abroad in and around the valley - like black dogs, dobs, hobs and lubber fiends[7]. Here, however, I shall consider reports from the upper Calder valley, and (mostly) save the lower reaches of the borough for another time.

Boggarty things were well enough known for the term to have had a wide usage. Inside houses, it was not only applied to poltergeist-like phenomena, such as furniture and other objects being moved around the house, or blankets being pulled off a bed, but also to other kinds of experience - the noisy hauntings, like knockings, that we may now think of as being caused by ghosts, or more prosaically structural 'settling' in an old house, were an indicator of boggart activity, as one story below attests. Anything mysteriously mischievous might well be ascribed to a boggart, though sometimes there is ambiguity as to whether a more frightening event is attributable to a boggart or a devil; this ambiguity is reflected in an old West Yorkshire limerick:

There was an old woman of Baildon
Whose door had a horse-shoe nailed on.
Because one night
She'd had such a fright
With a boggard that was a horn'd and a tail'd 'un[8]

Outdoors, a problem boggart might cause an accident, like a wheel falling off a cart, or lead a traveller astray. An expression, 'tekkin' t'boggart', was used locally if a horse shied in fright for no apparent reason, as it was and is thought that animals can see things which humans cannot (and would prefer not). The verb 'boggle', indeed, originally meant to take fright or shy like a startled horse, while a 'bogglish' horse - or, presumably, person - was one that was inclined to start at nothing, or at least nothing that anybody else could see. There was even a local verb, 'to boh', meaning to frighten.[9]

Horses didn't like the Haworth road, just above Pecket. Many a time there's a horse just stopped there and refused to budge, or took off in some other direction with no heed to the rider's call. There was one time when four horses together took boggart so bad they tipped up the whole cart they were pulling. They can see things that we can't, and they don't like boggarts at all.

One notorious area for horses to 'tek t'boggart' was on Cock Hill, between Pecket Well and Oxenhope; on one occasion, four horses pulling a laden wagon shied and overturned their heavy load. One of the two drivers had to go off and seek assistance, and it was reported that his companion was not too happy at being left alone with a danger that none but the horses could see![10] On some of these occasions, perhaps, carters might see a 'flame of fire' between the ears of their horses when they stopped suddenly, which surely implied the presence of a boggart.[11]

All in all, for the people who experienced such phenomena, whether it was a mischievous boggart, a spectral hound, a malicious witch or Old Harry himself was of little consequence - they just wished they'd 'boggart off' somewhere else and leave them alone. Other related words, like 'bogey', tend to reflect the less welcome character of these kinds of experience, and the *Oxford English Dictionary* gives further details of the family of words related to 'boggart'. Care must be taken, though, for one variant is 'boggard' - which in addition to meaning 'boggart' also exists as an old word for toilet, which gives us the modern 'bog'!

Some boggarts have particular affinity with houses or families, as 'The Cliviger Boggart' shows; it has been suggested that boggarts might even be seen as a kind of 'ancestor spirit'. Although they are rarely seen, perhaps the little man with a ginger beard seen at Boggart House in Cromwell Bottom in Brighouse was the resident boggart[12], as the description seems extraordinarily close to the traditional image of the kind.

Various Boggart Houses around the borough are testimony to this association; one below Midgley, known as such in the 17th century (it later became Ellen Royd), had in its garden a stone known as the Boggart's Chair. People said it had been worn into its hollow seat shape by a boggart sitting in it. This stone was eventually identified as the old font, with one side broken off, removed from the old Luddenden Church - the Boggart Chair can now be seen beside the altar in the current 19th-century replacement church[13].

There was a boggart at Mayroyd, that kept up a knocking and a banging through the night, and disturbed the people of the house a good while. But it went away after they'd drilled some holes in the underdrawing. And now they wonder if it was there at all.

It was thought that Mayroyd House in Hebden Bridge had acquired a boggart, when strange noises began to be heard in May 1859; but the suspected boggart was apparently 'laid' (as the expression goes for quietening a supernatural visitant) by drilling holes in the underdrawing![14] 'Antiquarian', writing in the Hebden Bridge Times around 1880, knew of a boggart at Hanging Royd[15].

Water-sites such as wells and bridges are also favourite places, and many a boggart and its kind has been encountered at old bridges in the valley; Kitling Bridge, which has been variously identified as the footbridge on the path from Pecket Well down to Midgehole and the more substantial bridge, also known as Hurst Bridge, at Sandy Gate above Hebden Bridge, which is actually a more likely haunt for such a tale. Another may be at Mare Hill in Warley, first recorded in 1624, which Smith attributes to "possibly OE *mare* 'a goblin, a spectre'" (as in *nightmare*)[16]. 'Fairy Well' field names are numerous, recorded by Smith in Sowerby, Soyland, Warley, Luddenden Foot, Sowerby Bridge, Mytholmroyd and Erringden.

> Dobbies are a funny kind of hob that seem to like farms, especially those where the farmer leaves out a dobbie stone full of milk or cream. That's a stone with a basin in it. Some people call them cats' troughs, and I suppose it just depends on who gets there first, cat or dob.

Other mysterious beings are found lurking in place-names, too - like the dob or dobbie (another mischievous sprite akin to the hobgoblin or hobthrust, as hobs were also known[17]) at Dob and Dob Lane in Sowerby, and perhaps Dobroyd in Todmorden, though 'dob' is also a local dialect word for the robin. There are other placenames that hint of a connection with the Other Folk, too, like Rishworth's Fairy Hill. Mytholmroyd had a Hob Lane, and Soyland, too; also in Soyland are Thurst House Farm, the name deriving from Thrust or Hobthrust, and the Awfe Hole. The latter, which had become Half Hoyle by 1833, was described by Watson as a kind of rocking stone, and by Leyland as apparently "the result of a settlement of the hill side which caused the slab that forms the cover of the passage beneath it, to slide from its former position"; Smith ascribes the name to Old Norse 'alfr' - elf[18]. Generally, however, elves were considered of a rather different order from the hobs and boggarts, so much so that they had a palace in Mytholmroyd - the now-vanished Elphaborough Hall was reputedly built where an elfin palace once stood, beside the Elphin Brook, as Cragg Brook is known as it passes through Mytholmroyd. 'Elphin', however, is probably derived from eels, rather than elves, but why spoil a good legend...[19].

But everywhere one hears that fairykind are loath to live alongside churches and mills: "Boggarts appear to have been more numerous when working people wove what was called 'one lamb's wool' in a day; but when it came to pass that they had to weave 'three lambs' wools' in a day, and the cotton trade arose, boggarts and fairies and feeorin of all kinds began to flee away from the clatter of shuttles"[20]. So if they are still with us today, perhaps the best places to find them may be some way away from the towers of religion and industry - like at the Boggart Stones, an atmospheric and evocative group of wind-worn stones above Widdop Reservoir, which seem welcoming enough whenever I visit them, but are said to be the home of a boggart that likes to torment passing walkers. Perhaps the key was not to tempt fate:

> Sam Fielden and Joseph Woodhead got on really well. Joe used to mend roads up and around Lumbutts, and betimes Sam would pass the time of day with his friend, and relieve Joe's labour by breaking up the odd stone. Well, one day, they were talking of this and that, and Sam remarked that he'd heard tell there was a boggart living thereabouts. Joe was a bit cautious in his reply "Well, Sam, that's so I've heard, but I can't say as I've seen owt". But Sam wasn't ready to let the subject go like that, and he asked his friend, rather carelessly it seems now, if the boggart were a white or a red one, and picked up a hammer to break one of Joe's stones. "I can't say as I've heard tell it's either..." But they were the last words he spoke to his friend, because as Sam swung the hammer, he just collapsed there and then and that was the end of him. Well, he was 50, and fond of a good meal, and it was his heart that gave out under the hammer, but local people said it was just too much of a coincidence, and it showed how you should always mind your words, and show respect, even if it were invisible.[21]

7. See Katherine Briggs, *A Dictionary of Fairies*, Allen Lane, 1976.
8. *Yorkshire Folk-lore Journal* Vol. 1, 1888, p.142.
9. 'Some Calder-vale Words', *Yorkshire Folk-Lore Journal* Vol. 1, 1888.
10. Rev. James Whalley, *The Wild Moor*, priv., Todmorden, 1869, p.23.
11. *Todmorden Times*, 26-12-1863.
12. *Evening Courier*, October 31, 1985.
13. Smith, *op. cit.*, p.133-4. Tom Sutcliffe, 'A Tour in Midgley', *HAS* 1928, p.117. A similar tale is told of another Ellen Royd, in Elland, which also had a Boggarts Chair in its garden, and was also known as Boggart House.
14. *Yorkshire Folk-Lore Journal* Vol. 1, 1888, p.2-3; *Todmorden & Hebden Bridge Historical Almanac* 1871, p.41.
15. 'Antiquarian', *Old Hebden Bridge & its People*, 1882, & 1991, p.18.
16. Smith, *op. cit.*, p.128.
17. From ON *þyrs* 'demon', Smith, *op. cit.*, p.188. A haunted bridge was known in the 16th century as Thir-

sley or Thrutchley Holme, while the Bay Horse Inn in Worsthorne, near Cliviger, was haunted by Old Thrutch. Tattersall Wilkinson & J F Tattersall, *Memories of Hurstwood, Lancashire*, Lupton, 1889, p.53-4.
18. Rev. John Watson, *The History of the Town and Parish of Halifax*, Milner, 1789, p.16; Leyland, F A. *The History & Antiquities of the Parish of Halifax*. Leyland & Son, Halifax, n.d., p.51; Smith, *op. cit.*, p.66.
19. Smith, *op. cit.*, p.160.
20. John Harland & T T Wilkinson, *Lancashire Folk-Lore*, 1882, repub EP, 1973, p.62.
21. John Travis, *Notes mainly of Todmorden & District*. Wrigley, 1896, p.300.

Threats and curses

Mothers used to tell their children to be good or the witches of Bog Eggs'd get them. 'Eggs' sounds like 'hags', you see, in the old way, but you know it really means 'edges', and right enough it's perched there on the edge of a bog. Anyway, I don't know where they got the idea, but they said these old hags would come at night to suck the blood of children who didn't behave. We never went up there till we got bigger! And then the people up there never seemed so fearsome, neither! As long as you behaved while you were on their land, I suppose.

More bogey characters were associated with Bog Eggs Farm, above Old Town in Wadsworth. It was reputed to be the home of some particularly nasty witches - well, rather demons or hags who were prone to suck the blood of naughty children at night. Despite the descriptive nature of the placename - the moor edges ('eggs') above the farm being very swampy - the local associations of 'Bog' with 'bogey' and 'boggart', and the close local pronunciation of 'eggs' and 'hags' probably helped the farmspeople to acquire their unenviable but unserious reputation. This piece of folklore turns up, surprisingly, in an English-Latin dictionary of 1552; Richard Huber wrote of "hegges or night furies or wytches (witches), like unto old women which do sucke the blood of children in the nyghte"[22]. It didn't seem to bother generations of thick-skinned farmers, though, until the 21st century, when more sensitive owners turned up and started to call it Allswell Farm! You'll still find it on the maps as Bog Eggs, as it's been known for centuries, and you'll still find the bog, too.

You'll not find more than a single rowan tree in Black Clough, not since them two Trawden women died there, must be a few centuries ago now. They fell down the clough side when it was snowing hard, and weren't found till after winter passed. One of them was still holding a rowan branch. She'd tried to hold on as she fell, but the feckless tree broke and killed her. Those that found her laid the curse on the tree that it'd never have a companion there.

It is said that only one rowan tree will ever grow in Black Clough, on Black Hameldon on the very edges of Heptonstall parish. This curse is attributed to the fate of two women, Isabella Shaw and Margaret Shuttleworth, who were travelling back across the moors to Trawden in 1689. As we have seen in our stories so far, the fickle Pennine weather plays a leading role in many of our local legends; these unfortunate women were among the many who have encountered a snowstorm in their travels across the moor, and among the number who perished as a result, slipping down the steep sides of the Clough and their bodies remaining there until the snow melted. One of them had obviously clutched at a branch of a rowan tree to break her fall, to no avail - the branch snapped, and down she went. It was still in her hand when she was found and the curse was laid on the 'treacherous' tree that no other of its kind would grow there[23].

Another curse is said to have afflicted a family - the Barcrofts of Cliviger's Barcroft Hall were condemned by a scion of the family, William, who allegedly was of an unstable disposition and was kept prisoner in the house by his younger brother, Thomas. An iron ring in the cellar of the house, and graffiti scratched in walls nearby, were pointed out as evidence of his travails. Evidently, someone in the household was more kindly disposed towards him, for one night he escaped from his irons; he was caught, but not before he pronounced a curse that his sibling's line would die out and the Barcroft lands distributed among other hands. Thomas' only son died the next year, leaving him without a male heir. William himself died of starvation in 1641; Thomas held on till 1668, but on his death the Barcroft lands passed on to his three daughters, and thus to their husbands' families. By 1700, there were no Barcrofts at Barcroft Hall[24].

You can never be too careful; when Hare Mill was built on Burnley Road in Todmorden in 1910, the imposing seven-storey redbrick cotton mill - locally criticised because it was seen as an intrusive blot on the countryside, as was then, and because it was built on a public fairground - attracted more criticism for its white hare running down the chimney, picked out in glazed bricks. The hare is an ominous beast, often said in the Pennines to be unlucky should one cross your path, and it is said that hares cannot run down steep slopes; thus, people said that depicting a hare running down a vertical face was a bad sign indeed. When the company ran into difficulties shortly after, the warnings about the power of symbolism seemed well-founded. The hare was removed when the mill, in line with contemporary events, was renamed Mons Mill; perhaps it was an attempt to counter the bad luck of the hare with some brand-new folklore of their time. The Battle of Mons in August 1914, between a small British expeditionary force and a massively superior German invasion army, was however a defeat for the British, and thus not the most obvious choice for a commemorative naming. Yet Mons went down in history for a different reason. What looked certain to become a terrible rout for the British forces was somehow averted when the Germans inexplicably halted their headlong advance. The British force was weak, demoralised and could not have saved itself, but something had to explain the inexplicable, and stories of supernatural salvation began to circulate. The soldiers were said to have seen a bright light in the air between themselves and the German army, and in the light appeared an armoured knight (whom many interpreted as St George) with a troop of bowmen confronting the enemy, or a host of angels confronting the German army. The Angels of Mons became one of the most celebrated legends of modern warfare[25]. Whether the renaming was intended as an angelic invocation or as a way or halting what seemed inevitable, it was unsuccessful in turning the mill's economic tide. Mons Mill was sold at the end of the war, and indeed was never fully built according to the original specifications. It was finally pulled down in 2000.

22. J H Ogden, A Moorland Township, 'A Moorland Township', HAS 1904-5, p.43.
23. Tattersall Wilkinson, 'Local Folklore' HAS 1904-5; Wilkinson & Tattersall, *op. cit.*, p.103.
24. Titus Thornber, *A Pennine Parish: the history of Cliviger*, Rieve Edge Pub., Burnley, 1987, p.64.
25. For a thorough and balanced investigation into the genesis and distribution of the powerful Mons legend, see David Clarke, *The Angels of Mons*, Wiley, 2004. For Mons Mill, see Issy Shannon, 'Mons Mill', *Milltown Memories* 5, Autumn 2003.

Making fun

Another way that places are commemorated is in the age-old tradition of derision. Communities everywhere have mocked their neighbours with names, rhymes and stories, sometimes in bad taste and perhaps uncomfortably close to the truth - Keighley folk, for instance, were called in the 18th and 19th centuries 'keighlegd'uns' (pronounced K-legged 'uns), because of the prevalence of rickets in the town. Such unflattering lore would to most people simply be annoying, but uttered in certain circumstances - such as when groups of young men were involved - it could well be seen as deliberate provocation for a fight, an aspect of local rivalry whose appeal shows little sign of abating, despite its institutionalisation into sports team support.

There is a celebrated local quatrain which I think sums this up:

Halifax is made o'wax,
Heptonstall o'stooan
In Halifax there's pretty lasses
In Heptonstall there's nooan

Which seems like nonsense until it is broken up into two associated couplets. Imagine two groups of lads facing off in the street: the Heptonstall lads shout

Halifax is made o'wax,
Heptonstall o'stooan

And the Halifax lads answer back:

In Halifax there's pretty lasses
In Heptonstall there's nooan

And in no time at all the rumble has been ritually instigated[26]! A similar rhyme that makes the point even more clearly comes from another part of the valley, where Elland and Greetland have evidently made an alliance:

Halifax is made o'wax,
Yelland's made o'steel;
Greetland's made o'knuckle-bone,
I challenge thee to feel.

Gauxholme, near Todmorden, was once known as Sodom, in a none-too-subtle reference to its reputation which would also seem guaranteed to provoke confrontation[27]. We have another local taunt about Walsden and Todmorden, which many will find fairly incomprehensible nowadays -

Heps and hages and hollin grubs
are fit for naught but Walsden cubs
Imber and blager nor other such prout
For which lads and lasses in Torm'den shout

Let's sort out the dialect first - 'heps' are hips, 'hages' are haws and 'hollin' is holly, while 'imbers' and 'blagers' are raspberries and blackberries respectively; 'prout' means rubbish, or something good for nothing. The first part of the rhyme is saying Walsden kids can be satisfied with unappetising and troublesome wayside food (they all need much preparation to become edible, which is why we hardly hear of them nowadays). The second part seems at first to suggest that only tastier and instant fare like summer fruits satisfy Todmorden youngsters, but this reading is complicated by calling such fruit 'prout'[28]. However, this little problem is solved if the rhyme is spoken aloud, when it becomes obvious that local speech patterns confused the man who wrote it down - the correct wording isn't 'nor other such prout', but 'not other such prout' (try it!), and it *is* a scurrilous Todmorden rhyme accusing Walsden kids of being country bumpkins with coarse tastes! It is perhaps better understood as a (seasonal) provocative taunt.

Todmorden itself features rather unfavourably in a story about Germany's Prince Bismarck, when he was resident in Manchester. He came across the town on a railway map, was struck by its name - which can be understood in the German language as a mixture of death and murder - and decided he had to see such a place. So he went off on the train, looked around the town, and came back to Manchester. On his return, someone asked what he had thought of Todmorden. "It matches its name" was his reported reply[29]!

Rivalry between communities, and the suspicion of strangers entering one's territory, was summed up by Heptonstall in the 1930s, according to the one-time editor of the *Todmorden News*, Sam Tonkiss. He remembered it as "a mediaeval village with a matching mentality. When a stranger entered the narrow street of terraced houses, a warning was sounded by rattling a poker on the fire-back and one's neighbour alerted. Within living memory visitors have been known to flee to escape a fusillade of a variety of missiles, mostly of a distasteful substance". He also recalled

Hebden Bridge men's disdainful term for Todmorden men as 'Ound yeds' (hound heads)[30].

The following 'Packhorse Litany' has appeared in numerous books on the history of upper Calderdale:

Burnley for ready money
Mereclough nooa trust;
Yo' takken a peep at Stiperden,
but call at Kebs yo' must.
Blacksha' yed for travellers,
an' Hep'nstall for trust;
Heptin Brig for lan'ladies,
an' Midgley by the moor.
Luddenden's a warm shop,
Royle's yed's varry cold;
An' if yo' git to Halifax,
yo' mun be varry bold.

It is a rhyme associated with the Long Causeway, the ancient road that might even date back to Bronze Age times, that runs along the northern slope of the valley from Burnley to Halifax. It is a long-established trading route and part of a network that stretched from the Irish Sea to the ports on Yorkshire's east coast. The highest point of this network and of this relatively easy passage between Lancashire and Yorkshire is the Calder Valley, and the rhyme advises travellers what to watch out for along the way. For instance, don't expect credit in Mereclough, look forward to good victuals at Kebs and an overnight stay in Hebden Bridge. But what do you really get in Heptonstall? Maybe you get the credit you were refused in Mereclough, but you certainly don't get the rhyme you have been led to expect! This bothered Donald Haigh so much that he was convinced that the Heptonstall line was rewritten for publications so as not to offend certain sensibilities of the period. He asked Sir George Clark for an opinion, and the Oxbridge professor suggested the original wording, which would satisfy rhyme and metre, might be 'whores' in place of 'trust', a suggestion I find convincing, and as Haigh remarks, "conjectural maybe - but with the ring of historical truth!"[31].

26. It has been suggested that the 'wax' referred to relates to the appearance of redbrick buildings, allegedly resembling sealing wax, in Halifax, but not so much in surrounding towns. As Halifax is such a handsome stone-built town, I find this a rather dubious explanation; but

then I have no other suggestion to make.
27. Travis, *op. cit.*, p.326.
28. Travis, *op. cit.*, p.255-6. This rhyme also demonstrates that the dietary role of wild food in the area was naturally wider than the bistort and nettles used in the well-known spring dish, dock pudding. Holly was more medicinal, as a purgative; but its leaves, dried and roasted, made a kind of tonic 'coffee'. I have found no evidence of hollin grubs - the larvae of the holly blue butterfly - being used for food, so have discounted this possibility.
29. Travis, *op. cit.*, p.345.
30. Sam Tonkiss, *Raking Amongst the Embers*, priv., Todmorden, 1987, p.21, 20.
31. Donald Haigh, 'Fax fallacies', *HAS* 1991, p.125-31. W B Crump, 'Ancient Highways of the Parish of Halifax', *HAS* 1924, p.65-126.

Stones and Stories

There is something about prominent stones that attracts folklore, as we have seen in the earlier chapters on Churn Milk Joan, the Bridestones and Great Rock. Others, like the Boggart Stones mentioned above, have smaller folkloric fragments attached to them, but still figure in the cognitive maps of their localities.

Two stones perch on the hillside above the Cat i'th'Well pub in Saltonstall, conspicuous because of all the stones on a rocky hillside, they are the only ones painted white. This happens every year, and has done so since The White Stones were first transformed around the beginning of May, 1890. That first time was probably connected with Spaw Sunday, the first Sunday in May and a day for people to flock to local mineral wells as a spring tonic. Of several in the area, the spring that emerged by the riverside in Luddenden Dean, a short way below the Caty Well bridge, was the most popular in the upper valley. The perpetrators of the custom - for such it has undoubtedly become - did not exactly keep it secret, but it *was* kept quiet, helping tales to form; in 1905, Whiteley Turner, who called it White Rock, wrote "It was never discovered who did it. What is more, though the rocks ever since have periodically received a fresh coat, no one has been caught with brush and pail"[32] . Some said it was the landlord of the pub, and one tale went so far as to bring Robin Hood into the story, saying that he had once been hidden at the inn when on the run, and needed to conceal his booty. He struck up an arrangement with the landlord, and they buried the treasure beneath the rocks; subsequently, in return for a share of the proceeds, the landlord painted the stones white each year to signify to Robin or his spies that the hoard was safe. Well, many dates

The White Stones, looking towards Wainstalls

have been put forward in attempts to historicise the legendary outlaw, but to date none has suggested the 1890s as Robin Hood's heyday! One year, it is said, the stones were painted pink instead of white, and later that year the pub went out of business[33]. Another story has it that an ancient chieftain and his treasure are buried beneath it[34], while a member of the Mytholmroyd Historical Society in 2000 had heard that they were painted white by the Devil on New Year's Eve. I have been told personally, by another member of the Mytholmroyd society in 2000, that the painting was carried out, at least for some time, by a family who lived in nearby Wainstalls, but that they had since moved; my informant did not know if they still carried on the custom or if it had passed on to someone else.

Further upstream from the pub in Saltonstall is Nunnery Farm, known as such since around 1598; nearby is Catherine House, and Caty Well (from which the Cat i'th'Well inn name comes - or is it the other way round?), which speculation occasionally suggests may have been a holy well dedicated to St Catherine. Local tradition has had it that some of the nuns expelled from Kirklees priory at the Dissolution retired to the area, and also that there used to be a church in Saltonstall, so Nunnery Farm, first recorded not so long after the Dissolution, may recall their habitation and place of worship; among the Kirklees nuns was an Isobel Saltonstall, so the possibility cannot be entirely ruled out[35].

At Stones, above Todmorden, stands a monolith that is the fourth tallest standing stone in Yorkshire. Almost nothing is known about this stone, aside from a few notes made at the end of the 19th century, which suggest that the stone was found recumbent and re-

The standing stone at Stones, above Todmorden; Flower Scar Hill in the background

erected on the spot to commemorate the Battle of Waterloo. The then owner of nearby Stones House, Samuel Greenwood, was said to have been involved; a prominent local Quaker, he subscribed to the building of the first Stoodley Pike, and it might well be that the stone was raised to celebrate not the battle, but the peace that followed it. Smaller standing stones in nearby fields have been suggested as sighting stones[36]. Nearby is a certainly modern standing stone on the hilltop, which was erected as a beacon, possibly again as an act of commemorating the peace.

> We used to go up on the moor and go round the Keb Stone nine times if we had the breath, chanting, because we thought we'd raise the giant if we did it right. Not that we ever did, so we used to say we must have done it wrong, or maybe the giant was away visiting his mum or something like that.

A massive block of millstone grit on Moorhey Flat, above Walsden, is known as the Keb or Kemp Stone, and is said to be one of a pair; the other one lies among Shaw Stones, on the other side of the valley on Knowl Top Edge. Like Robin Hood's Pennystones in Midgley and Wainstalls, it is said to have been thrown across the valley by a local giant - in this case, Old Chedley Redcoit, so named because his coat was all stained with the juice from the bilberries that he loved so much. Children held that if you went round the stone nine times, chanting 'Chedley, Chedley Redcoit' all the while, you would call the old giant up and he'd chase you away[37].

The Greenwood Stone; the date, 1775, may have been cut during a boundary perambulation by pupils of Heptonstall Grammar School, of which there is some record around that time.

The final stories in this section relate to modern times on Midgley Moor. These are not traditional tales, at least not yet; but they are local stories associated with specific places, and they contain the kinds of ideas and experiences that may well have fed into the tales that have come down to us. They both reflect and reiterate a perception of Midgley Moor that strange things can happen there, a perception that is clear also in the stories told of Churn Milk Joan and Miller's Grave. Does the Moor itself inspire such stories? Or is it just big enough to accommodate all human imagination?

The Greenwood Stone, on the old Wadsworth/Midgley boundary, was recorded in the boundary documents of 1598 as lying down, and so it remained until 1976, when a group of young men decided to put it back up again. They did a good job, as it's still standing, but the work - performed in the dark hours, as they did not wish to be seen - was attended by strange experiences like flashing lights and psychic disturbances; for one of the men, the mental disturbance continued for some time afterwards. The event as it was described to me sounded very similar to a 17th century account of magic rite in which the conjured spirit appears where it shouldn't: "the sign of their appearance will be very delectable and pleasant, though various and amusing the senses to behold, as a shining brightness, or sudden flashes ...all about or in the place where action is made"[38]. Things seem rather calmer around the stone nowadays.

The other modern tale is a strange one indeed, and I do not know what to make of it at all. It must be said that I heard it in a pub - always the primary venue for sharing, even creating, folklore, but in this case the story had and retains a different 'aura' to it from most pub tales[39]. It related to a time during the 1970s, when many people were moving into the valley and renovating derelict properties to make a new life in the Pennines. Among them were two men doing up a property on the Heights Road below Midgley Moor:

> *I tell you, I've heard of some strange things happening up on that moor, and some I'd rather not have heard at all. There was a lot of talk in the pub about thirty years ago, after a couple of fellers doing up a house along the Heights Road cleared out without finishing it. I was told that one of them had come in to the pub one night, right shaken up, and he told a gruesome sort of tale, and that was the last they saw of him. Seems he and his mate had been up on the moor above their house when they saw a kind of rippling coming across and through the heather at 'em. Well, they looked, and they saw, and - well, just talking about it chills me to the bone. It was rats, what they call a march o'rats, and it was coming towards them. Well, the one that came into the pub that night told the other to stay put, don't move, just let 'em pass; but he didn't or couldn't do that, and ran. And the rats had him, so he said, and they chewed him up, down to the bones. The other one, you know, he didn't have much heart in living round here after that, and left. That's what they say, anyway - funny, though, that I never read about it in the papers. You'd think that something like that would make the news. So I can't really believe it - but then there must be something behind a story like that, mustn't there?*

I have been unable to get any more information on this incident, and it is hard to imagine such a story escaping the news media, or indeed investigating agencies, if it really happened. Nonetheless, 'a march of rats' is apparently an expression for when a community of rats decides to migrate, and does so *en masse*, on a ratty whim. My informant said they were coming from Hebden Bridge Station goods yard, though where he got that idea I have no idea. Whether such a rat pack can turn murderous to humans is a similar unknown, but this kind of behaviour is apparently known in stoats, as one Yorkshireman attested in the 1930s. A number of stoats "leaped at him... snapping little white fangs"; he fought back with a stick, knocking some into the ditch, and kicked off some whose teeth had fastened into his trouser legs, but as he fought them off, they returned to the attack until he took to his heels. In this case, staying put would not have seemed wise. A naturalist in Burnsall was also once frightened away by an aggressive stoat pack, while a driver near Thurso watched as a large stoat pack crossed the road in front of him, apparently on some purposeful journey. Other accounts of experiences with stoat packs sound so similar to the Midgley Moor tale that perhaps it is not so unlikely a tale after all.[40]

32. Whiteley Turner, *op. cit.*, p. 44.
33. *Malcolm Bull's Trivia Trail*, online directory of Calderdale local history & other information, now discontinued. Accessed November 20, 2003.
34. Andy Roberts, *Ghosts & Legends of Yorkshire*, Jarrold, 1992, p.6.
35. 'Notes on Luddenden', *Hebden Bridge Times* August 2, 1882; Smith, *op. cit.*, p.128.
36. Abraham Newell, *A Hillside View of Industrial History*. Priv., Todmorden, 1925, p.34.
37. John Travis, *Round About Todmorden*, Chambers, Todmorden, 1890, pp.21-2.
38. MW, pers. comm. Dr Rudd, q. in Adam McLean, *A Treatise on Angel Magic*. Phanes Press, Gt Rapids, MI, USA, 1990, p.173-4.
39. Kim Parkinson, August 2003.
40. Merrily Harpur, 'Stoat Packs'. *Fortean Times* 214, Sept. 2006, pp.39-41

There are many other tales that relate to places, that are harder to group into category. A quaint story tells that when John Fielden was courting his working-class weaving-maid girlfriend, and they were out walking on the edge of the hills above Todmorden, he enquired of her where she would like to live after they got married. She had already told him she'd like to live in a castle, and now she stopped, bent down and picked up a stone. Throwing it hard and high - she was a mill-girl after all, no effete bourgeois - she watched where it fell, and said "there". And that's how Dobroyd Castle came to be where it is. In fact, once she moved into the mansion, she could not settle, and disliked the house so much she left it.

A bridge in Shade, Todmorden, is known as Gurning Dog Bridge, after a nearby pub. The inn was actually the White Lion, but its inn sign did not manage to exactly capture the essence of the lion, and gave rise to its nickname of the Gurning Dog.

Noah Dale, upstream from Colden, has given its name to a song, 'The Noah Dale Anthem'. It may not originally be a local song - Harry Greenwood remembered it being named as such because of an occasion when it was sung at the Kettledrum Inn in Mereclough by a number of Noah Dale men coming back from beating at a grouse shoot at Hurstwood. A *Hebden Bridge Times* reporter was present at the sing-song, and bestowed its name in his report. Bert Dobson's version of the story, however, has it that the Noah Dale men at the Mereclough singaround were asked if they had any 'anthems', and one replied "aye, we've got the Noah Dale anthem"[41,] and so it became.

Ghosts and hauntings are also invariably associated with places, and especially pubs; but to start getting into them here would extend this volume too far, so we will leave them for another time. Accounts and place-names of Robin Hood, too, abound in the Calder valley, which is generally accepted as the place of the legendary outlaw's death, at Kirklees Priory: but Robin's local associations must wait till the next volume of this collection.

Of course, these are not the only stories to be told of Calderdale, and I look forward to coming across more. There are folk tales that are not tied to any particular place, for instance, and there must be local by-names and reputations attached to places that have yet to be recorded.

Moreover, there are many tales that might be told of memorable historical events. Invariably, amongst such spectacular episodes, certain crimes figure strongly - such as the murder of Sammy o'Katty's at Hawden Hole in 1817, or Miles Weatherhill's frenzied attack on Todmorden vicarage in 1868, or even the 'grandaddy' of them all, the 14th century saga of malice and revenge known as the Elland Feud. These documented historical events, however, fall outside the scope of this collection, which has concentrated on those stories that have come down to us at a certain remove from what we like to call reality - but which were, at a certain narrative level, a reality in which local communities lived.

---

41. Harry Greenwood, (ed. Bob Pegg), *Memories*. Arvon Press, 1977. Mary & Nigel Hudleston, *Songs of* *the Ridings: the Yorkshire Musical Museum*, Pindar & Son, 2001, p205 & 323.

Endwords

All over the world, traditional stories tend to repeat certain clear motifs, and those in this book are no exception. Folklorists Antti Aarne and Stith Thompson separately produced indices of these common elements, which have been combined into the Aarne-Thompson index of types and motifs.

For the record, these are some of the motifs we have encountered in this collection of folktales; further constituent motifs can be recognised by consulting the Index, or Ernest W Baughman's updated *Type & Motif Index of the Folk-Tales of England and North America* (Indiana Univ. Press, 1966):

A972.2.2 The devil's footprint;
D100 Transformation: human to animal;
D142 Transformation: human to cat;
D702.1.1 Cat's paw cut off: woman's hand missing;
D1381.22 Mist separates person from companions;
D1418.1 Mist causes people to get lost;
D1641.2.4 Stone moves at midnight;
D1642.2.4(a) Stone turns around on its base at midnight;
D1901 Witches induce love;
E334.2 Ghost haunts burial spot;
E411.1.1 Suicide cannot rest in grave;
E412.3 Dead without proper funeral rites cannot rest in grave; E431.16 Burial of suicide to prevent walking;
E431.16.3 Suicide buried at crossroads;
E431.19 Burial of corpse at midnight to prevent walking;
E441 Ghost laid by reburial;
E501 The Wild Hunt;
E501.4.1 Dogs in a wild hunt;
E501.18 Evil effects of meeting the wild hunt
E782.1 Hands restored;
F261 fairies dance;
F263 Fairies feast;
F361 Fairy's revenge;
F361.17 Other punishment by fairies;
F482.3.1.1 Farmer is so bothered by brownie that he decides he must move - brownie comes too;
G211.1.7 Witch in form of cat;
G211.2.4 Witch in form of deer;

G252 Witch in form of cat has hand cut off. Recognised next morning by missing hand;
G275.12(bcb) Person cuts paw off cat; witch has hand missing;
G275.2 Witch overcome by helpful dogs of hero;
G303.4.5.3 Devil has horse's foot;
H1233.1.1 Old woman helps on quest;
N571 Devil (demon) as guardian of treasure;
N828 Wise woman as helper;
T110 Unusual marriage.

The folklore, custom and tradition of a district is a vital statement of its identity, and of all aspects of local history provides the most eloquent description of its culture and character.

I am preparing a number of other works on this aspect of Calderdale, including a further volume of local legends, and would be pleased to hear of other lore and tradition, from children's games to contemporary ghosts, work initiation ceremonies to fairy haunts, etc., relating to the area. (Please state whether you would like your name to be used in any resulting publications or not).

I can be contacted as follows:

John Billingsley, c/o Northern Earth Books, 10 Jubilee Street, Mytholmroyd, Hebden Bridge HX7 5NP

Or email: editor@northernearth.co.uk (mark messages FAO John Billingsley)

By the same author:

A Stony Gaze: investigating Celtic and other stone heads (Capall Bann, 1998)

The Day the Sun Went Out : accounts of the 1927 solar eclipse in Yorkshire (Northern Earth, 1999)

Aspects of Calderdale (ed.) (Wharncliffe Press, 2002)

The Mixenden Treasure (Northern Earth, 2008)

A Laureate's Landscape: Ted Hughes' Mytholmroyd (Northern Earth, 2007)

John Billingsley is also editor of *Northern Earth*, a quarterly journal of neo-antiquarianism, archaeology and folklore.

www.northernearth.co.uk

INDEX

Ambry Well 68
Baildon 70
Barcroft Hall 75
Barkisland 66
Bearnshaw Tower 10-18
Becket, Thomas á 67-68
Black Clough 74-75
Blackshaw 39-43, 66, 79
Blackstone Edge 67
Bog Eggs 74
Boggarts 19-22, 47, 65, 69-73, 74
Bridestones 23-29
Brig Races 43
Brighouse 71
Bronze Age sites 53, 59, 61
Burnsall 85
Chedley Redcoit 82
Choppy Knife Mill 49
Churn Milk Joan 55-63
Churn Milk Peg 62, 63
Cliviger 14, 19-22, 74, 75
Cock Hill, Wadsworth 70
Colden Valley 67, 68, 86
Cornholme 10-18
Cragg Vale 58, 72
Cromwell Bottom 71
Devil 34, 39-43, 66, 67, 81
Devil's Rock 39-43, 66, 67
Dobroyd 72, 85
Dragons 64-66
Druids 28
Dule Hole Bank 67
Dulesgate 67
Eagle Crag 10-18
Elland 73, 77, 81, 86

Ellen Royd, Elland 73
Ellen Royd, Luddenden Foot 71
Elphaborough Hall 72
Elves 72
Erringden 72
Extwhistle 21
Fairies 21, 30-32, 72, 73
Fast-Ends 28
Fielden, John 85
Folly Field, Midgley 63
Freemasons 33, 36-37
Gabriel Ratchets 15
Gauxholme 77
Goldsmith's Grave 53
Greenwood Stone, Midgley 61, 73
Greetland 65, 77
Grisly Stone 43
Halifax 52-53, 59, 68, 77, 79
Hallowe'en 10, 15
Hanging Royd, Hebden Bridge 72
Hardcastle Crags 44-49, 86
Hartshead 65-66
Haslam, Michael 54, 60
Hathershelf 47
Hawden Hole 86
Hebden Bridge 43,50,68,71-72,78-79,84
Hebden Hey 47
Hell Hole Rocks 49
Heptonstall 49,50,53,61,74,75,77,78,79
Hermits 69
High Brown Knoll 61
Hobs 72
Hobthrusts 72, 74
Hughes, Ted 43, 55, 60
Jack-in-Irons 47

89

Keb Stone 82
Keighley 77
Kirklees Priory 81, 86
Langfield 30, 36
Larkmen 43
Long Causeway 79
Lubber Fiend 21, 71
Luddenden 53, 69, 71, 72, 77-78, 79
Lumbutts 30, 36, 37, 73
Mayroyd, Hebden Bridge 43, 50, 71
Mereclough 79, 86
Midgehole 72
Midgley 50-63, 71, 79, 82-85
Miller's Grave 50-54, 61
Mons Mill, Todmorden 75-76
Mount Skip 50, 56, 68
Mytholmroyd 48, 61-62, 67, 72
Nelmires 61
Noah Dale 86
Old Harry Lane, Mytholmroyd 67
Old Town 27, 74
Old Woman 17, 26
Ovenden 65
Packhorse Litany 79
Parkinson Lane, Halifax 52-53
Pecket Well, 27. 67-68, 70, 72
Pendle Witches 16, 65
Pennystone 58-59
Portsmouth 10-18
Preston, John 69
Ripponden 35
Rishworth 67, 72
Robin Hood 53, 58-59, 65, 86

Robin Hood's Pennystone 53, 58, 61, 82
Rowley 21
Royle's Head 79
Saltonstall 80-81
Savile's Low 61
Shade 85
Sleepy Lowe 37
Sowerby 61, 72
Sowerby Bridge 72
Soyland 72
Stansfield 23-29, 66
Staups Moor 39
Stiperden 79
Stones, Todmorden 81
Stoodley Pike 15, 33-38, 39-42, 67, 82
Stubbing Wharf 43
Suicide 50, 52-54
Thieveley 12, 17
Todmorden 23-30, 72, 75-78, 85, 86
Tom Bell 44-49, 65
Trawden 74-75
Tuel Lane 67
Uffington White Horse 42-43
UFOs 38
Wadsworth 27, 61, 67-68, 74, 83
Wainstalls 59, 81
Walsden 30, 77-78, 82
Warley 37, 72
White Stones 80-81
Widdop 73
Wild Hunt 15
Worsthorne 21, 74